Sanctified Vision

An Introduction to Early
Christian Interpretation of the Bible

John J. O'Keefe and R. R. Reno

The Johns Hopkins University Press
Baltimore and London

© 2005 The Johns Hopkins University Press
All rights reserved. Published 2005
Printed in the United States of America on acid-free paper
9 8 7 6 5 4 3 2

The Johns Hopkins University Press
2715 North Charles Street
Baltimore, Maryland 21218-4363
www.press.jhu.edu

Library of Congress Cataloging-in-Publication Data

O'Keefe, John J., 1961–
    Sanctified vision : an introduction to early Christian
interpretation of the Bible / John J. O'Keefe and R. R. Reno.
        p.   cm.
Includes bibliographical references and index.
ISBN 0-8018-8087-4 (alk. paper)
ISBN 0-8018-8088-2 (pbk. : alk. paper)
1. Bible—Criticism, interpretation, etc.—History—Early church,
ca. 30–600. I. Reno, Russell R., 1959– II. Title.
BS500.O39 2005
220.6'09'015—dc22
2004022317

A catalog record for this book is available from the British Library.

Sanctified Vision

For our parents,
JoAnna O'Keefe and John J. O'Keefe, III,
Mary Ellen Reno and Russell R. Reno, Jr.,
With gratitude

Contents

Preface

This joint project was the result of the somewhat random character of office assignments. For more than ten years we have been neighbors. For a greater part of that decade we have been in each other's offices, flopping down in a chair and blowing off steam about our mutual dissatisfaction with contemporary theology and its hopeless modernisms, or sharing moments of classroom success when we seemed to have communicated to our students the striking density of Christian thought. Over the course of those years, one issue came into focus for both of us: the role of biblical interpretation in the logic of Christian theology. We were dissatisfied with the stock categories of "liberal" and "conservative." Neither seemed accurate to describe how most of the influential figures in Christian history actually thought—neither were satisfactory for our own sense of our vocations as Christian theologians.

We came at this insight into the centrality of biblical interpretation from different angles. John O'Keefe was trained in patristics. Rusty Reno studies modern Catholic and Protestant theology and ethics. These seem like fatally disjunctive categories, but one of the most significant benefits of the predominantly undergraduate focus of Creighton University where we teach is the freedom to explore outside one's specialty and offer courses at the border (some might worry beyond the border) of one's competence. John designed a course called Scripture and Theology. Rusty began to teach it. The occasional conversations became regular. Unfocused dissatisfactions and random successes began to jell around a common theme of early Christian biblical interpretation. This book was born.

The providence of office assignments may have brought us together, but a raft of influences brought our minds to maturity on the topic of ancient Christian biblical interpretation. For John, the interest in patristic exegesis goes all the way back to his first years of graduate study. Brian Daley's seminar on patristic Christology provided a point of entry into the discipline and raised questions about the relationship between the "schools" of Antioch and Alexandria that continue to provoke. Robin Darling Young's courses on patristic exegesis at the Catholic University of America made it abundantly clear that traditional patristic scholarship had largely neglected patristic texts devoted to biblical interpretation. From these influences came a dissertation and a series of articles. These in turn produced a growing sense that the academic conversation about patristic interpretation of the Bible was stuck in a rut. In one way or another, basic assumptions about the relationship between Antiochene and Alexandrian styles, the inviolability of historical criticism, and the methodologies of the fathers controlled all academic discussion of patristic interpretation. Discussion of these control points varied from author to author, but no study seemed able to step back from this basic vocabulary to gain a larger perspective on the fathers' approach to the Bible.

For Rusty, the interest in the fathers' interpretive practices came at the end of a long pilgrimage through the wreckage of modern theology. A product of the so-called Yale School, Rusty was socialized into the mysteries and eccentricities of postliberal theology. The effect was an inability to accept modern theology as a normal science. But where should one turn if one thought Jürgen Moltmann pointed toward pious temporizing rather than a viable form of Christian reflection? George Lindbeck penned the oft-quoted line: the text absorbs the world, not the world the text. How could a follower of Lindbeck move beyond incantation and toward an analytically precise account of such an affirmation? Slowly, the church fathers came into view as the proper object of study, for they were the original midwives of absorption.

Both of us have countless people to thank. Rusty has already mentioned one of his teachers, George Lindbeck, and chapter 1 pays homage to another of his teachers, Hans Frei. They are the two presiding presences whose influence transcends the tradition of prefatory thanks. Two Yale friends were more immediate in their guidance of Rusty's movement toward the church fathers. David Dawson is the most creative reader of Origen currently writing. His recent book *Figural Reading and the Fashioning of Identity* had an incalculable influence. In Dawson's hands, the reading practices of the church fathers were integrated into their vision of salvation. The work of Ephraim Radner defies epitome, but the fabric of his many publications is woven with figural patterns of biblical interpretation. He is a rare contemporary practitioner of an ancient art.

At a more pedestrian level, Dawson and Radner assign readings. They both are likely to say, "You have of course read . . ." Dawson forced a rereading of Erich Auerbach and a reconsideration of the legacy of Hans Frei. The crucial assignment was Auerbach's remarkable essay "St. Francis of Assisi in Dante's *Commedia*." Reading Radner is an exercise in being reminded of what you do not know. He is the guardian of the memory of theologians forgotten by the modernist history of theology that dominates contemporary academic study. His transformative reading assignment was the Anglican gem, John Keble's Tract 89, *On the Mysticism Attributed to the Early Fathers of the Church*.

John owes much to the work of Frances Young. Her essays and books on the interpretive practices of the fathers and the relationship between Alexandria and Antioch forced into clear view the difficulties inherent in how we have tended to talk about interpretation in the early church. None of this has been a substitute for immersion in the actual texts of the fathers. Disciplined habits of reading were a key feature of the Early Christian Studies program at Catholic University. The long hours spent poring over texts with Robin Darling Young, Bill McCarthy, and Thomas Halton have left a strong mark on this work. While Rusty was rereading Frei and Auerbach, John read them for the first time. They, along with Lindbeck, helped him to think differently about how to approach ancient reading.

As with Rusty, John's friends have left their mark. He extends gratitude especially to Stan Rosenberg and Ken Snyder, who have endured years of musing on the subject of the Bible and the fathers. Meetings of the North American Patristic Society, especially the informal conversations, have been a great source of insight and stimulation. That gathering of scholars bears eloquent testimony to the continuing power of the fathers to fascinate and compel.

As we worked to produce drafts of *Sanctified Vision*, we benefited from our students' comments. Rusty must thank the students in his spring 2003 section of Theology and Scripture. They worked through Ireneaus' *Against the Heresies*, Origen's *On First Principles*, and Augustine's *On Christian Doctrine*. John must thank the graduate students in his fall 2003 section of Inventing Christianity. They read an early draft of the manuscript and helped us clarify crucial points and make it more readable. We also need to thank the folks at Crane Coffee on Cass Street in Omaha. We provided them with money, and they offered us caffeine and a table to help us through the many long hours of discussion and rewriting.

Colleagues and fellow laborers in the bountiful vineyards of patristic interpretation commented on various stages of the manuscript. David Yeago, Stanley Hauerwas, Peter Martens, and Peter Ochs read the manuscript and lent encouragement. Robert Wilken provided helpful advice for revision, though we must beg his indulgence for our continued distinction between typology and allegory.

Sanctified Vision

CHAPTER ONE

Scriptural Meaning
Modern to Ancient

Day after day, day after day
We stuck, nor breath nor motion;
As idle as a painted ship
Upon a painted ocean.

S. T. COLERIDGE, *The Rime of the Ancient Mariner*

Reading the church fathers is difficult. Simply to pick up Irenaeus' treatise *Against the Heresies* and read invites confusion and boredom if one does not know the point of the many digressions. Most of them involve biblical details, either as misread by his adversaries or arranged as so many bricks in Irenaeus' seemingly endless wall of defense. History books told us that Irenaeus was important because he linked the idea of apostolic succession to the continuous public ministry of bishops and identified the authority of the rule of faith. So, as first-time readers, we dutifully soldiered through page after page, underlining here and there when he seemed to be saying something that fit with what we were told. Vast stretches of text seemed irrelevant to these issues; they were veritable wastelands under titles helpfully provided by a patient nineteenth-century translator: "Proofs in continuation, extracted from St. John's Gospel"; "Futility of the arguments adduced to demonstrate the sufferings of the twelfth aeon, from the parables, the treachery of Judas, and the passion of our saviour"; "Explanation of the words of Christ, 'No man knoweth the Father, but the Son,' etc; which words the heretics misinterpret"; and so forth. We did not so much thirst for righteousness as hunger for what we imagined to be the red meat of doctrine.

The same held for more familiar texts. Both of us remember taking up Athanasius' *On the Incarnation* for the first time. A twentieth-century translation, often reprinted, is prefaced by C. S. Lewis' winsome commendation that begins with an exhortation to read old books. We hardly needed encouragement, for we have been long convinced that old and dusty books in dead languages carry the romance of antiquity. "Let Time be your editor" was our watchword. Yet, good intentions do not always produce good results. Athanasius' treatise is far more focused and less rambling than Irenaeus', but our first, second, and third readings were oblique rather than direct. We could read portions, especially the richly theological chapters, but what were we to do with the larger balance of chapters that seemed an undifferentiated mass of biblical citations?

Even so familiar a figure as Augustine seems to have written in a fashion we were untrained to read. The first nine books of his *Confessions* have a strong narrative structure, telling the story of his life until the death of his mother. Moreover, the use of the first person voice has so saturated our cultural consciousness that Augustine's story of his soul has an immediacy that makes the book accessible in our own time. Nonetheless, in places we found our eyes glazing over. The first paragraphs of the *Confessions* are a striking address by Augustine to God that states the argument of the book as a whole. We might sum it up as follows: "The Lord should be praised, but how can sinful flesh come before the face of God? Alone I will fail, but God is with me. God's grace will triumph." Yet, this summary is really false to these opening pages. The initial paragraphs are not a statement of theme; they are a tissue of biblical quotations spoken in and given continuous form by Augustine's own voice. He never sums up, as we might wish he had, to clarify the point of this rhetorically extended scriptural preamble to his narrative. Once again in our reading, it was the biblical idiom of patristic literature that was most opaque.

Theological students and historians have ways of managing the discomfort caused by the great bulk of the patristic use of the Bible. For the most part the strategy is to change the subject. The standard textbooks tell a story about early Christian theology that centers around the great creeds and councils, emphasizing the interaction of patristic theology with the philosophical idioms of antiquity.[1] In recent decades this approach has been expanded to include study of the social structures in which patristic thought developed and to which it contributed.[2] Social history now compliments intellectual history. Thus, a student can pick an introductory history book off the shelf and learn that Athanasius' *On the Incarnation* is a crucial text in the formation of a Trinitarian consensus that Jesus Christ is the incarnate Son who is *homoousios* with the Father.[3] At a more advanced level, students might read a monograph discussing the role of Neoplatonism in the thought of Gregory of Nazianzus and thus see how the famous slogan "That which is not assumed is not redeemed" gains cogency in light of certain metaphysical assumptions.[4] The same holds for more postmodern concerns. One can read about Athanasius or Gregory and how their treatises, commentaries, and letters outline a regime of ascetical discipline of the body.[5]

We were grateful for the sophistication and guidance provided by the expansive literature of modern patristic scholarship. The only problem is that the emphases of so much modern scholarship—doctrine, metaphysics, and sociocultural practices—seem oddly out of focus in the actual texts of the early church. The church fathers wrote all manner of books, as one would expect given the differences of cultural milieu, occasions for writing, and, of course, personal sensibilities. We have letters both private and public. We have treatises on doctrinal topics and treatises addressed to present controversies. We have homilies and commentaries. We have collections of sayings from desert monks, poems, colloquies, and dialogues. Some wrote in Greek, some in Latin, others in Syriac. Some evidenced a flair for speculative thought; the minds of others ran in a more practical, concrete direction. No doubt, at times, the vast array of patristic literature comes into focus around doctrinal, metaphysical, and sociocultural issues. Athanasius' argument in the opening chapters of *On the Incarnation* is elegantly constructed upon the premise that the identity of God permits no inconsistency between creation and salvation. One can nearly smell the Platonism on the pages of Origen's work, and there can be little doubt that the church fathers were quite consciously seeking to build up and buttress the moral and spiritual disciplines of the church. Nonetheless, it is biblical citation, paraphrase, and exegesis that underlies all the diversity of patristic literature as the great common denominator.

We saw the vast ocean of exegesis, and yet we did not see it. We recognized that most early Christian writing is saturated with biblical particularity, but as we continued to think in terms of doctrinal development, intellectual context, and social systems, the actual exegesis remained obscure and unanalyzed. Slowly we became unsettled and dissatisfied. It was as if we began to tire of the study of the oceangoing arts that focused on the development of ship technology, the ways in which military needs shaped maritime practice, the schemes for organizing crews, and the mechanisms for capitalizing shipping companies.

We began to find ourselves unable to rest with the equivalent of studies such as *Studies of the British Royal Navy: 1723–1763,* or *Rum Runners and Slave Traders: Colonial Boston Merchant Firms,* or *Throats Unslaked: The Rime of the Ancient Mariner as an Allegory of the Modern Thirst for Meaning,* or *Whips of Leather: Sex and Discipline in the Venetian Navy of the Fifteenth Century.* We increasingly worried that we did not adequately understand the vast ocean of biblical sensibility upon which all the particular forms of patristic thought and practice floats.

The spur from within our reading of patristic literature bit sharply on a number of occasions. How many times must we read and teach Origen's *On First Principles,* a dauntingly speculative inquiry into the nature of God, the world, human existence and destiny, before noticing that the opening sentence stipulates that the Bible is the sole source of wisdom? To see that sentence and understand its meaning is like receiving a blow to the head. If we are to take him at his word, we must suppose that Origen thought that the entire sweep of his speculative theology had its sole source in the Bible. If this is so, we must either allow that Origen did not know his own mind—a conclusion implausible on its face—or get on with the business of explaining how he could make such a claim about the Bible. Here, we were brought up short. The logic of the assertion would seem to lead to the conclusion that Origen's speculative theology is an exercise in exegesis. We were utterly incapable of expounding this conclusion because we could not see how Origen made good on this claim. We were not equipped to see and understand just how his theology is exegetical.

It is Origen's gift that he brings his thought to a level of conceptual abstraction that allows his readers to see the consequences of his project. Once Origen had opened our eyes, we realized that a great deal of our failure as readers of patristic theology had to do with our inability to grasp the exegesis of early Christianity. We struggled through chapter after chapter of digressive biblical analysis in Irenaeus because we did not have the slightest idea what he was doing. The same held for much of extant patristic literature. Were we to put the often-read doctrinally oriented treatises next to the volumes of largely unread patristic commentary and homily, the latter would dwarf the former.

To recognize our ignorance was the first step. Soon, we sought guidance. We turned to the growing scholarly literature that seeks to shed light on the interpretive practices of early Christianity. By and large, this literature tells a story of historical context and development.[6] For example, the Jewish tradition of exegesis shaped Christian reading, and this tradition interacted with the Hellenistic rhetorical traditions. Prophetic Jewish reading of scripture, evident in the Dead Sea manuscripts, is clearly present within the New Testament's use of the

Old Testament. The Greek rhetorical use of allegorical interpretation to expound Homer's epics influenced Christian readers, expanding the resources for Christian reading that were instrumental in the preservation of the Old Testament against Marcion's proposal to reject its authority. We could go on, for there are countless threads to trace backward and forward.

We learned much about the history of patristic exegesis, but we still felt incompetent to read and understand it. Knowledge of origins and development gave us little insight into the actual practice. To know that Origen is a great and influential representative of the Alexandrian school of exegesis, and to know that this school was shaped by Neoplatonic ideas already present in the pre-Christian Jewish community of that city, and that these ideas endorsed ambitious allegorical strategies of interpretation could not help us understand *how* Origen read. To know that he was an indefatigable allegorist gives no insight into the logic of allegory. The actual structure and motive of patristic exegesis continued to elude us.

What was the method of patristic exegesis? What was the goal of their allegories? How did the fathers engage the specific details of the text? How did figural or typological exegesis, often highlighted by scholars as distinctive to the Christian tradition, function? What controlled and guided the seemingly arbitrary exegetical moves? Historical surveys and monographs could not answer these questions, which added up to a broad and crucial question for us: How did the fathers read? We wanted to get inside their interpretive world and see how they constructed their exegesis.

This book is the fruit of our efforts to understand the structure of patristic interpretation of scripture. It is not concerned with the history of exegesis. We do not try to identify schools or influences or to track regional differences between the exegetical practices of the church fathers. To know the history of patristic exegesis is not the same as knowing *how* that interpretive tradition functions with its own inner logic and cogency. Our purpose is to consider the exegesis itself as a discrete intellectual practice. We wish to engage and analyze the ocean upon which theological battles of doctrine were fought and across which the merchant trade of institutional life was conducted. That ocean is the great body of patristic exegesis.

History Lessons

Our desire to understand patristic exegesis does not preclude or discount historical study. The history of exegesis provides crucial background for investigation of reading techniques. To know the context and precedents can help one identify the crucial elements of interpretive practice. Furthermore, knowing the history can prevent the blindness that often comes from importing anachronistic assumptions into an analysis of the past. Ironically, the history most important to this project is not ancient but rather the history of our inherited, modern assumptions about biblical exegesis. We were incapable of reading the church fathers because of our own assumptions about how the Bible ought to be read. Our assumptions about what is meant by literal and spiritual, as well as our notions about the relationship between doctrine and scripture, made the church fathers seem disorganized, ineffective, and even contradictory.

For example, in his arguments against Gnostic interpreters of scripture, Irenaeus consistently denounces their symbolic reading of various numbers in the Bible.[7] Yet, Irenaeus himself provides a symbolic interpretation of why there are four gospels. He claims to demonstrate the necessity of the four and only four gospels because of the fittingness of the number four. The gospels symbolize the four zones of the world and four principle winds, which, in turn, points to the universality of the gospel and the spirit of truth that the church teaches, "breathing out immortality on every side, vivifying men afresh."[8] Because we tended to assume that exegesis must be controlled by a set method that either rules out or permits the use of number symbolism, we were back to our familiar position—what is he doing? Is Irenaeus confused, unable to see how he is contradicting himself? Does Irenaeus not use the same method of number symbolism? How is Irenaeus doing anything different from the willful allegorical interpretation for which he so vigorously criticizes the Gnostics?

Irenaeus is not unique. In our first encounters with the church fathers, we had difficulty seeing any consistent method of reading. Sometimes they commended literal readings, then embarked on an extended allegorical interpretation, all the while criticizing others for a lack of properly disciplined exegesis! A classic example of this puzzling lack of methodological clarity is Augustine's *Literal Commentary on Genesis,* in which much of his interpretation is not at all literal, at least not according to our assumptions about literalness. The same odd use of the term *literal* and the disorienting shifts from the historical idiom of certain biblical passages to moral exhortation to theological speculation characterizes most patristic exegesis. Even in the more restrained and sober Antiochene school of exegesis that opposed adventurous allegory, exegetes trafficked in these shifts.[9]

For us, then, the first step toward understanding patristic exegesis was a moment of self-criticism. We began to realize that it might be our anachronistic assumptions about the meaning of the terms *literal* and *spiritual* that made the fathers seem obscure, not some defect in their interpretive assumptions. For this reason, a history of modern exegesis, a history of our own interpretive presuppositions, was as important as the many historical studies of patristic exegesis. We turned to some studies of modern interpretive theory.[10] From them we learned important lessons.

As naïve readers of patristic exegesis, we had difficulty seeing how assumptions about meaning governed the logic of exegesis. We were fixated on method. We assumed that approaches such as source or redaction criticism defined modern historical-critical reading. As we read more deeply in the church fathers, this confused us. We could see that figures such as Origen seemed aware of some of the basic techniques of text criticism, techniques at the core of modern study of the Bible; yet, his exegesis was wildly different from modern interpretations. Nobody picking up a commentary by Origen would think it contemporary. The same odd conjunction of similarity and difference can be found in Augustine. He discusses the importance of cultural and historical context for the proper interpretation of the polygamy of the patriarchs in Genesis.[11] Yet, this sensitivity to historical context, one of the essential modern themes of biblical interpretation, appeared to have no influence upon the great bulk of his exegesis. We did not understand why similar techniques produced such different results.

Slowly, we began to realize that the key issue rested in our preconceptions about what is significant about texts, preconceptions that we had inherited and that motivated our use of technical strategies such as source and redaction criticism. Modern scholars have developed critical techniques for reading the Bible because they wish to more adequately assess the link between ancient events or experiences, and the scriptures that they take to be the record or representation. This need to assess and judge the link between text and its supposed referent emerges because modern readers assume that the Bible is important evidence for the subject matter it seeks to communicate. Origen and Augustine may have anticipated some of the technical strategies used by modern readers, but their whole approach was different. They made different assumptions about the meaningfulness of the scriptural text.

In order to adequately explain this difference, we need to be clear about the dominant modern assumptions about meaning. On a very basic and nontechnical level, these assumptions specify just why a word, sentence, or text is important. One might say, for example, that a biography of George Washington is important because it is accurate in its many details or because the author provides a convincing narrative that captures the "spirit of Washington." These are two very different reasons for wanting to read the biography. In the first case, we are motivated to read because we think the biography accurately represents actual events, intentions, and experiences. In the second case, we trust the biographer's more impressionistic portrayal of Washington because we believe that it conveys the spirit of the time or the larger interplay of ideas and influences that made him so important in American history. This difference is significant; however, what unifies the two approaches is a common assumption about meaning. In both cases, the biography is important because we judge it to be an effective vehicle or sign for what really matters: either the actual facts of Washington's life or the larger themes and movements that he embodied.

At a more technical level, the assumptions that we find so influential in the modern context tend to solidify into a theory about how words, sentences, symbols, narratives, and so forth work to communicate what is important. Most modern readers hold a referential theory of meaning, which assumes that our words and sentences are meaningful insofar as they successfully refer or point. So, we can say that the biography of Washington refers. We call the biography good because we think it accurate. We can argue about how to assess accuracy. Some hold to the supreme importance of the facts of history. Others think that a biography should evoke the subject's larger personality or world view. Nonetheless, this is a debate united by a common referential theory of meaning. The Washington biography is good insofar as it successfully refers to or communicates the subject matter, the particular x considered to be important.

We need to be clear that the referential theory of meaning does not settle any important or interesting questions about just how to characterize the subject matter to which texts refer. There can be continual discussion about just what the x might be, and the modern study of hermeneutics should be understood as an ongoing debate about this issue. The more empirical side argues that words and sentences should be best understood as referring to facts or states of affairs in the world. The more phenomenological side of the debate finds this position too simple-minded and draws attention to how texts convey the consciousness or experiences of the author. Nonetheless, the common referential theory of meaning gives an overall structure to the modern approach to interpretation.

One should adopt reading techniques that help one proceed from what the text says to what it seeks to represent. Reading is an act of movement from understanding the words to comprehending the facts and events (the empiricist preference) or ideas and experiences (the phenomenological preference) that the words seek to communicate. To use a spatial metaphor, a referential theory of meaning encourages us to read out of the text and toward the true subject matter to which it seeks to refer.

Modern biblical study is shaped by the modern theory of referential meaning. The Bible is significant because it refers. The Bible has an *x*, a subject matter, and good interpretation helps readers shift attention from the signs or words to the *x* that is the real meaning of the signs and words. For example, modern scholars assume that the gospel stories matter because they tell of the life, teachings, and deeds of Jesus of Nazareth. Of course, most modern readers can see that the gospel stories do not refer directly. They do not read like a detailed modern biography, firmly supported by citations from memoirs and other documents of the day. The lack of clear historical accuracy is even more evident in the historical narratives of the Old Testament. The story of Abraham and his descendents, the story of Moses and the exodus of the Israelites out of Egypt, as well as the stories of the kings of Israel, do not refer in any straightforward way. All the narratives in the Old and New Testaments have layers of tradition and are shaped by the cultural contexts of their composition. Moreover, they are clearly composed to serve communal, religious interests. They are not "historical" in the sense of intending to provide a dispassionate, objective account of personalities and events.

Once modern readers see the distance between what the biblical stories say and what likely actually occurred, the distinctive reading strategies of modern historical-critical reading become important. A technique such as source criticism seeks to unpack biblical texts and show the different layers of composition, some of which stem from certain time periods and communities, and others of which come from different eras and serve different interests. A well-known fruit of this approach is the distinction between the Priestly and Yahwist material in Genesis. Equally important are the attempts to organize the material in the three synoptic gospels into different source traditions that likely predate the composition of the canonical gospels. This effort should be understood as modern scholars trying to create a body of material that can function as memoirs, letters, and primary documents function in the writing of a modern biography. Assuming that the gospel stories, like all texts, are meaningful insofar as they succeed in capturing or referring to their subject matter, scholars set out to find sources by which we might discern whether or not the received texts do in fact succeed.

For us, the plausibility of the modern scholarly analysis that has produced these hypotheses is not at issue. What is important is how the referential theory of meaning motivates modern reading strategies. Modern readers of the Bible assume that, as in a biography of Washington, the events to which the scriptural narratives refer is what makes them important. Because the biblical accounts of history are so opaque and so different from scholarly histories, we are motivated to adopt reading techniques such as source and redaction criticism in order to refine our interpretation and, in this way, catch some glimpses of "what really happened."

Not a few modern scholars either were pessimistic about the possibility of reading the Bible as a source of information about actual historical events or were inclined to think that religious truths have an ideal and not historical form. In our case, when we thought about the narratives in Genesis and Exodus, we did not feel the need to determine the historical accuracy of the stories. We did not read the story of the exodus or the ascent of Moses onto Mount Sinai as garbled accounts of historical events, so we did not need to look for possible sources and provide detailed assessments of the historical reliability of various details. Instead, we assumed that the narratives communicated a religious meaning. To discern it, we attempted to draw out the theological structure or symbolism. We read the stories as disclosing or pointing to theological truths about God's saving purpose. For example, we might have said that the meaning of the episode on Mount Sinai is best understood as a vivid narrative portrayal of the basic biblical truth that God initiates the covenant with his people in the act of sovereign command. Salvation comes from God alone. In this approach, the text does not refer to historical events; it refers to important theological or doctrinal propositions. The actual details of the story or the sequence of the words on the pages are not important. What matters is the religious or theological idea the text represents.[12]

For a long time we were stuck at this point. We imagined that a concern for the historical reference of the Bible defined modern historical scholarship, and we thought that our theological readings represented a different approach. Of course, they are different, much as the biographer of Washington who seeks detailed accuracy differs from the biographer who tries to shape the material into a narrative that captures the spirit of Washington. Yet, the underlying, referential assumptions about meaning are the same. Whether reading the text to find out what really happened or to gain access to theological principles, the Bible's meaning depends upon tracing the arc of representation out of the words and into the subject matter. Like too many modern readers, we were inclined to show that the Bible can serve as a body of evidence for what really happened or, in our case, for theological propositions. Thus, no matter how differently modern interpreters assess the subject matter of the Bible or its religious significance, there is a united front. The Bible is important in light of its capacity to refer to some x—what really happened or timeless truths.

To our surprise, our views about the Bible's meaning were not held by premodern readers. Premodern readers assumed that events depicted in the Bible actually occurred as described, but surprisingly little of their interpretation depended on this assumption. They simply did not ask: "What is the event or truth to which the Bible refers?" For them, the text was woven into the fabric of truth by virtue of being scripture. As Irenaeus affirmed, "the scriptures are indeed perfect, since they were spoken by the Word of God and His spirit."[13] For Irenaeus and for the patristic tradition in general, the Bible was not a perfect historical record. Scripture was, for them, the orienting, luminous center of a highly varied and complex reality, shaped by divine providence. It was true not by virtue of successfully or accurately representing any one event or part of this divinely ordained reality. Rather, the truth rested in the scripture's power to illuminate and disclose the order and pattern of all things.

As a consequence, in patristic exegesis literality functioned as the basis for interpretation. Scripture certainly did refer, evoke, symbolize, exhort, command, and more. In all these particular instances, the fathers took the text as doing something that reached beyond the literality of the words. The words of the synoptic gospels pointed to events such as the life and teachings of Jesus. The opening verses of the Gospel of John referred to truths about the divine Word. The ten commandments represented God's will for human beings. The list could go on and on, but the important point is that the fathers treated all these aspects as local phenomena. Treated as a whole, the Bible absorbed their attention rather than directing it elsewhere, either to the events to which the text refers or the divine truths to which it points. Scripture was the magnetic pole of their thought. In this way, the fathers differ from modern readers, not in any particular assumption about a verse or episode, or in any specific method, but in their overall assumptions. Modern readers assume that the Bible means by accurately referring to an x, whether event, mode of consciousness, or theological truth. For the fathers, the Bible is the array of words, sentences, laws, images, episodes, and narratives that does not acquire meaning because of its connection to an *x;* it confers meaning because it *is* divine revelation. Scripture is ordained by God to edify, and that power of edification is intrinsic to scripture.

The image of *direction* illuminates the difference we discovered in the fathers. Ancient readers of scripture moved within, across, and through the text, exploring its orienting, unifying potency. Modern readers of scripture move in the reverse direction, adopting techniques that lead out of what seems a confusing, inaccurate, and contradictory text and into a realm of history or theological ideas. Thus, premodern readers are rightly called precritical, not because they presumed the historical accuracy of scripture or because they failed to use the various techniques of critical analysis that characterize modern study of the Bible. Rather, they are precritical because they did not ask, "What gives meaning to the story of Moses' ascent of Mount Sinai?" They assumed the authority of the dual accounts in Exodus and Deuteronomy, and they sought to order their interpretations accordingly. Instead of looking behind the text to the events, they looked into the text for clues and solutions.

For example, the fathers noticed that the gospels of Matthew, Mark, Luke, and John differed in detail, but this did not prompt them to look for the "true Jesus" behind the text. Instead the texts themselves provided the tools for reconciling the differences. The scriptures were treated as the context for divine meaning, the perfect language that instructed even in its apparent difficulties and imperfections. On this point, Origen testifies to the basic sensibilities of the church fathers. "If anyone ponders over the prophetic sayings with all the attention and reverence they deserve"—for Origen, the whole of scripture has a prophetic structure—"it is certain that in the very act of reading and diligently studying them his mind and feelings will be touched by a divine breath and he will recognize that the words he is reading are not utterances of man but the language of God."[14] Thus, for the church fathers, what scripture does in any particular verse or episode, which may entail presuming reference to historical events or intentions or theological ideas, was very much a matter of debate. However, Origen and the rest of the patristic tradition presumed, as their tacit theory of scriptural meaning, the importance of the words themselves. To know the words is prior to and more decisive than knowing if they refer and to what. Scripture is at the center of reflection. This assumption is the foundation of patristic exegetical practice.

The precritical presumption that the meaning of scripture is in the words and not behind them explains why modern readers find patristic exegesis so unfathomable. We read ancient commentary and seek to discern the *x* outside the text that governs the exegesis of the fathers. Some are inclined to think the key is their "literalism" that credulously assumes that the text provides reliable reports of actual historical events. Others tend to focus on doctrines, and they imagine that patristic exegesis is an extended effort to prove the truth of orthodox teachings by matching up scriptural verses with creedal propositions. Neither approach works because both assume that something akin to the modern theory of meaning as reference—either to history or to doctrinal propositions—animated the exegetical practices of the fathers. As we plan to demonstrate, if we stop anachronistically projecting the referential theory of meaning onto the fathers and accept that precritical interpretation of scripture presumes that the text *is* the subject matter, then patristic exegesis can be understood as a tradition of interpretation that makes sense on its own terms.[15]

A Patristic Illustration

We hope that our analysis of the church fathers' particular reading strategies will provide sufficient evidence of the value of setting aside modern assumptions about meaning. At this point, however, the distinction between modern assumptions and premodern assumptions may still seem obscure. In fact, for many readers, our description of the precritical assumptions can seem impossible. How can the meaning of the text be found in and through the text? Would this approach not entail an empty and intellectual morbid capitulation to the scriptural inerrancy? What is left for an interpreter to do if the text is exalted at such a high level? These are questions that theoretical reflection is unlikely to satisfy. An example might help.

Gregory of Nyssa was one of the Cappadocian fathers who lived in Asia Minor and wrote in the fourth century. Gregory's theological and exegetical writings, like his brother Basil's, are often regarded as a high point in early Christian thought because they integrate the sophistication of ancient Greek philosophy into the structure and idiom of Christian orthodoxy. This integration is evident in his *Life of Moses,* a treatise that follows the ancient technique of inviting readers into the pursuit of wisdom by portraying a great man who prefigures the path of truth seeking. In this account of Moses, Gregory considers many episodes. We want to focus on his account of Moses' successful contest against the magicians of Pharaoh's court. Gregory's interpretation is based on Exodus 7:8–12. The scriptural text reads as follows.

> And the Lord said to Moses and Aaron, "When Pharaoh says to you, 'Prove your-selves by working a miracle,' then you shall say to Aaron, 'Take your rod and cast it down before Pharaoh, that it may become a serpent.' " So Moses and Aaron went to Pharaoh and did as the LORD commanded; Aaron cast down his rod before Phar-aoh and his servants, and it became a serpent. Then Pharaoh summoned the wise men and the sorcerers; and they also, the magicians of Egypt, did the same by their secret arts. For every man cast down his rod, and they became serpents. But Aaron's rod swallowed up their rods. (RSV)

What Gregory does with this text reflects his own theological vision of the Christian life. Here, however, we want to focus on the features of his exegesis. These features are typical of the patristic era and provide a striking illustration of the difference between precritical and critical theories of meaning.

Gregory divides his account of Moses' career into two sections. The first he calls *historia*. In this section, he does not question or reconstruct an account of "the historical Moses." Instead, he consolidates material from Exodus, Levi-ticus, Numbers, and Deuteronomy in order to produce a continuous narrative of Moses' life. Here is a taste of Gregory's sense of *historia*, which involves a summary account of Exodus 7:8–12.

> Pharaoh (for this was the Egyptian tyrant's name) attempted to counter the divine signs performed by Moses and Aaron with magical tricks performed by his sor-cerers. When Moses again turned his own rod into an animal before the eyes of the Egyptians, they thought that the sorcery of the magicians could equally work miracles with their rods. This deceit was exposed when the serpent produced from the staff of Moses ate the sticks of sorcery—the snakes no less! The rods of the sorcerers had no means of defense nor any power of life, only the appearance which cleverly devised sorcery showed to the eyes of those easily deceived.[16]

A modern reader trained to read critically can easily see that Gregory's synopsis takes liberties with the particular details. He assimilates Aaron's actions with Moses', and he interpolates homiletic judgments about the episode's meaning. We have heard similar retellings from the pulpit over the years. What is most striking, however, is not that Gregory expands on incidents in Moses' life that serve to maximize the rhetorical impact on his readers but that he seems to call this exercise "history." Gregory makes no effort to probe the veracity of the events or to reconstruct the true nature of Moses' encounter with Pharaoh. The words on the page are the subject matter of his "history," which he rearranges in order to serve his homiletic goals.

The difference between Gregory and us is not that he was naïve and we are not. The difference is more fundamental. He simply did not ask what Moses' life was *really* like. No doubt he assumed the depictions of the Pentateuch corresponded to real events. However, the word *historia*, which is the etymological source of the word *history*, can be linguistically deceptive. Both words imply narrative sequence. For us history is the sequence that the narrative refers to, and we query the accuracy. In contrast, by *historia*, Gregory never meant a reconstructed life of Moses conceived as a truth alongside and in competition with the text. His *historia* is a rhetorically motivated reconstruction of the scriptural narrative, designed to make the episodes depicted in scripture more accessible to the reader. It is, we might say, a Cliff Notes version.

The second part of the *Life of Moses* underscores the difference between modern approaches and the patristic approach. There, Gregory interprets the *theoria* of the text. *Theoria* is a technical Greek term he adopts to describe the spiritual sense of the scriptures. The best English equivalent for the term *theoria* is *contemplation,* but in patristic literature it also often functioned as a virtual synonym for *allegoria.* By the time Gregory was writing in the fourth century, the term *allegory* had become suspect, in large part because it was associated with Origenist theological speculations that were eventually condemned. Thus, Gregory adopted the term *theoria*, avoiding the dangers of associating himself with allegory and the Origenist positions.

At the outset of the second half of his *Life of Moses,* where he begins his exposition of the *theoria* of the text, Gregory puts forward Moses "as our example for life." Gregory gives the impression that the *theoria* is a catalogue of virtues exemplified by Moses' life, something like what we might encounter in popular religious literature where pious authors search the scriptures for spiritual nuggets that one suspects were lined up in advance. In other words, we might think Gregory assumes a version of the modern theory of meaning: the text refers to or directs our attention toward some x, spiritual truths that are independent of the discrete verbal reality of the passage.[17] Some of what he says seems to follow this pattern. For example, in the *historia* the infant Moses, though adopted by the princess, is nursed by his own mother. From this episode, Gregory draws out a piece of Christian wisdom: "This teaches, it seems to me, that if we should be involved with profane teachings during our education, we should not separate ourselves from the nourishment of the church's milk, which would be her laws and customs."[18] However, Gregory's approach to the *theoria* does not fall neatly into this pattern of linking episodes in the *historia* with spiritual truths. What has been crucial for us is the recognition that, on the whole, Gregory finds the *theoria* within the literal, verbal details of the text. The narrative details are not irrelevant to Gregory's *theoria* as they tend to be for modern readers mining for spiritual truths.

The episode of Moses' rod becoming a snake illustrates. Joining together Exodus 4 and 7, Gregory offers a spiritual interpretation of the meaning of the miraculous change. The transformation is, he writes, "a figure of the mystery of the Lord's incarnation, a manifestation of deity to men which effects the death of the tyrant and sets free those under his power."[19] The change in substance from staff to snake directs attention toward the crucial change in substance that is at the center of Christian teaching: the Son of God becomes man to conquer the devil and release us from our captivity to sin and death. Yet, Gregory does not rest with a theological conclusion, as if the passage somehow refers to Nicene doctrine. His analysis turns toward the verbal or literal clues in the text.

He first observes that we should not trouble ourselves with the use of the image of a snake as a type for the Son of God become man, "as if we were adapting the doctrine of the incarnation to an unsuitable animal." Gregory sees his teaching confirmed by scripture itself, "for the Truth himself through the voice of the Gospel does not refuse a comparison like this in saying: And the Son of Man must be lifted up as Moses lifted up the serpent in the desert [John 3:14]."[20] Gregory turns to the New Testament not to prove that this episode in Exodus refers to the doctrine of incarnation but in order to reflect on the fitness of using the image of a serpent to understand Christ. The serpent image in Exodus reminds him of another serpent image in John. Gregory is moving across the text of the Bible, not past it.

Of course, John 3:14 is an echo of Numbers 21:9, which tells of Moses' use of a bronze serpent raised on a staff to protect the Israelites from the affliction of poisonous serpents sent by the Lord to punish them for their faithlessness. The serpent in Numbers has nothing to do with the context of Exodus. One is bronze and affixed to a staff; the other is a staff turned to a serpent. Gregory is nonplused. The image in Numbers is filtered through John, and Gregory takes it to illuminate the significance of the serpent in Exodus 7.10. The issue, then, is not a strict parallelism of transformation from rod to serpent deployed as evidence to prove the doctrine of incarnation. Gregory does not assume that the text is a vehicle that points or refers to something outside its verbal structure. He does not treat scripture primarily as a medium through which to discern spiritual patterns, likely historical events, or the intentions of the biblical authors. Although he will, in many places, emphasize each of these aspects as he sees fit, the appeals to reference are ad hoc. He does not push through or beyond the text to reach its "true meaning." Instead, Gregory is following the purely verbal clue of the canonical use of *rod* and *snake*. He is intensifying the text as the key to its own interpretation.

As his exegesis moves forward, Gregory's concentration on the literal or verbal clues in scripture is striking. Led by purely literal suggestion, he restates the *theoria* of the text in the idiom of rods and serpents, drawing together diverse scriptural verses into a series of inferences.

> The teaching is clear. For if the father of sin is called a serpent by Holy Scripture and what is born of the serpent is certainly a serpent [John 8:44, Rev 20:2, Gen 3:1], it follows that sin is synonymous with the one who begot it. But the apostolic word testifies that the Lord was made into sin for our sake [2 Cor 5:21] by being invested with our sinful nature. This figure therefore is rightly applied to the Lord. For if sin is a serpent and the Lord became sin, the logical conclusion should be evident to all: By becoming sin he became a serpent, which is nothing other than sin. For our sake he became a serpent that he might devour and consume the Egyptian serpents produced by the sorcerers [Ex 7:12]. This done, the serpent was changed back into a rod by which sinners are brought to their senses [Prov 13:24, 1 Cor 4:21, Rev 2:27], and those slackening on the upward and toilsome course of virtue are given rest [Num 20:11], the rod of faith supporting them through their highest hopes [Ps 23.4].[21]

However we read this exegesis of Exodus and the episode of Moses' staff, it is difficult to imagine that Gregory is seeking a meaning in anything to which the text might refer. The *theoria* of the text is not a stock or inventory of spiritual truths represented or symbolized by the text. Words such as *snake* and *rod*, as well as patterns such as the miraculous transformation of substance, combine with Gregory's own mental inventory of crucial Christian disciplines to suggest connections with other scriptural verses that are arranged in a web of exposition.

We have claimed that precritical readers did not separate the depictions, idioms, and verbal structures of the Bible from their subject matter; rather, the meaning of the text was sought within the text. Gregory bears out this claim.

His *historia* is an artful retelling of the material about Moses in the Pentateuch, shaped by what Gregory assumes are the parameters for a proper heroic biography. It is not a reconstruction according to historical judgments about an actual sequence and structure of events. The *theoria* is a web of scriptural associations, no doubt guided, consciously or unconsciously, by Gregory's sense of the overall unity and shape of Christian truth, but constructed across and within the literal detail of scripture. As he reports at the end of his prologue to the *Life of Moses,* his goal is to discern the spiritual meaning that corresponds to the *historia,* and the latter simply is the distinctive sequence and verbal reality of the scriptures themselves.[22]

We remain modern readers, and we have no interest in denying that the historical circumstances of the composition and Gregory's distinctive theological vision shape the *Life of Moses.*[23] A great deal may be learned if one inquires into the nature of that vision and the antecedent influences that shaped it in Gregory's mind. Furthermore, we are eager to affirm that the technical vocabulary Gregory adopts, as well as the interpretive techniques he uses, has interesting and important histories. We have indicated that he has reasons for using *theoria* rather than *allegoria* to describe his second, spiritual stage of exegesis. These circumstances and more formed the milieu in which Gregory was educated and worked. Yet, these important historical facts are for naught if we fail to understand how Gregory read. When we impose modern assumptions about meaning, we cannot see that he ordered his exegesis centripetally. The arrow of analysis is directed toward and through the literal particularity of the text and not beyond it. If we are willing to entertain this mode of analysis, however alien its assumptions, then we believe it is possible to enter into biblical interpretation of early Christianity and understand some of its characteristic modes of interpretation.

Our Plan of Analysis

In this study, our overriding goal is to explain how the arrow of exegetical analysis moves toward and through the biblical text. To understand the patristic strategy, we propose a straightforward approach. We try to expound in some detail representative portions of patristic exegesis. Our object is not to identify historical antecedents or to discern the extrinsic reasons *why* the church fathers interpreted the Bible as they did. Instead, we wish to discern the structure or logic operating within early Christian interpretation. To do so, we do not conform to a developmental model of explanation. The specific portions of patristic exegesis have been selected on the basis of an analytic scheme, according to their capacity to illustrate certain reading techniques that we hope to explain. Our hope is that this analytic approach will allow us to illuminate the particular ways of reading that the church fathers adopted in order to expound the meaning they presumed to be intrinsic to the text. Our approach is organized around three basic strategies of textual analysis: intensive, typological, and allegorical.

These strategies make up the core of the book, but we do not want to give the impression that any of the three are "methods" in the modern sense of the word. As we shall argue in the final chapter, the fathers saw their reading as disciplined, but unlike modern intellectuals, they did not focus on method or technique as the key to reliable or accurate analysis. They did not carefully distinguish between different modes of reading, nor did they feel it necessary to restrict their exegesis to one approach. In any extended portion of interpretation, the fathers might use intensive strategies while pursuing a larger, allegorical reading. A typological reflection might blend into an allegorical scheme; a brief allegorical digression might play a role in a developed typological interpretation. Therefore, we need to emphasize that intensive, typological, and allegorical reading are categories we have isolated for the sake of our analysis of the fathers' rich and varied exegesis.

The intensive reading strategy is a broad category that ranges from philological analysis that is indistinguishable from aspects of modern biblical study to word associations that are utterly alien to the critical sensibilities of contemporary readers. Across the range, however, we identify a common patristic focus on the particularity of biblical language, an almost sensual attempt to engage the words of scripture. We have already seen this at work in Gregory's analysis of the *theoria* of Exodus 7:8–12. There, he used the literality of the words *rod* and *serpent* to build a network of verbal associations that operates within the larger scheme of his attempt to discern the *theoria* of the life of Moses. We further unpack this strategy of intensive focus on specific words and word sequences in chapter 3.

The second strategy is figural or typological interpretation. The terms *figura* (Latin) and *typos* (Greek) are widely used in ancient literature, but the technical term *typology* and sustained analysis of what is entailed in this interpretive approach is not part of the ancient tradition. By and large, the church fathers spoke of allegorical or spiritual interpretation more generally. During the Reformation and after, Protestant scholars were concerned to reinforce what they took to be the plain or literal sense of scripture. As a result, they coined the term *typology,* and they sharply distinguished it from allegory, arguing that the former rightly operated within the literal atmosphere of scripture, while the latter entailed a willful abuse of the literal sense. This distinction supported Protestant arguments against Catholic biblical interpretation. Modern scholars have adopted a similar sharp distinction between allegory and typology, sometimes to establish a bridge between modern historical-critical study and ancient typological exegesis, and at other times to advance theories about the unique humanistic aesthetic inaugurated by Christianity.[24]

We adopt the term *typology,* but we do so without assuming a sharp distinction from allegory. For us, it designates a ubiquitous patristic interpretive practice that discerns patterns within and between discrete events depicted within scripture. An interesting example of the link effected by figural reading can be seen in Theodoret of Cyrus' interpretation of Psalm 29, a psalm about a thunderstorm.[25] Theodoret, following most of his peers, was eager to map the Psalms on the historical time line of the book of Kings. Theodoret presumed that because the Psalms were the "Psalms of David" they had to do with his life. Following other ancient exegetes, he connects Psalm 29 with events described in 2 Kings (4 Kings LXX) 19:35–36, where Hezekiah is delivered from the Assyrians. In this reading, Psalm 29 is linked to actual events out of Israel's past.

As we have noted, the idea that scripture refers to historical events is affirmed by the fathers. That they did not regard the historical events as the foundation for scriptural meaning did not prevent them from discussing historical references. However, as Theodoret explains, the historical reference is not the end of the story: "On the one hand this psalm fits the time of King Hezekiah. But, on the other hand, it is about the king of us all who eradicates the error of idolatry and who illuminates the economy with rays of divine knowledge." The psalm refers to Hezekiah's victory; it also refers to Christ's lordship and triumph. This link is developed as Theodoret arranges the details into a pattern of typological correspondence: "In the old the king is pious, in the new Christ is the teacher of piety. In the old the people are encouraged by the king, in the new the people are saved by him. In one there is war and destruction of the Assyrians, in the other a rising up against and liberation from demons."[26] The result is not a focus on the primary historical referent for the psalm. Instead, Theodoret sets up an ordered correspondence between the psalm, an episode in 2 Kings, and the presumed sequence of redemption in Christ. Ancient events are connected to present events and practices. The connection itself seems to carry the weight of meaning. In the fourth chapter we examine how the patristic tradition established figural connections of this sort.

The third major strategy is allegory, the topic of chapter 5. As we have noted, allegory is not conceptually or essentially distinct from typology. It is an extension of the typological strategy that does not limit itself to discerning patterns of and between events. Allegory is more fluid and ambitious. It seeks patterns and establishes diverse links between scripture and a range of intellectual, spiritual, and moral concerns. The literature on allegory is dauntingly complex, both in ancient times and today. Our goal is not to try to do the impossible, which is to explain or justify the odd capacity of the human mind to discern and exploit patterns at many different levels in both texts and reality. Instead, we hope to show how allegory functioned for the church fathers within the literal environment of the text.

Gregory of Nyssa's *Life of Moses* is a treasure trove of examples of the different strategies of patristic exegesis, including allegory. His analysis of the *theoria* of Exodus 28, which contains a lengthy description of the vestments worn by the high priest, illustrates the allegorical approach.[27] Because Gregory believes that Moses was privy to spiritual revelation, he assumes that these details have an enduring spiritual and allegorical significance. Nonetheless, the significance is very difficult to discern. He is particularly interested in a passage that discusses the placing of the "Urim and Thummim" in the "breastpiece of decision," the blue color of the vestments, and the adornment of the vestments with bells and pomegranates (see Exodus 28:30). To gain some purchase on the meaning of these obscure textual details (modern scholars are as baffled by the Urim and Thummim as was Gregory), Gregory focuses on the purpose of the vestments. They are to be worn as Aaron goes before the Lord to hear the word of judgment.

Gregory presumes that God judges according to his doctrine and truth. For this reason, Gregory is motivated to think through the ways in which the Exodus depiction of Aaron's vestments can be understood as describing qualities of the soul that will prepare us to come before the judgment seat of the Lord. The garments described in Exodus 28 are "not the perceptible clothing which is traced by the history but a certain adornment of the soul woven by virtuous pursuits."[28] The Urim and Thummim on Aaron's breastplate are the doctrine and truth of God that we should keep always on our hearts. The tunic's blue dye, the color of the air, represents our ascent toward the light of God. The golden bells and pomegranates are the "brilliance of good works," pursued through faith and good conscience. The pomegranate's hard casing and ordered interior represent the philosophical life, which appears harsh but hides an ordered beauty.

Contemporary readers may find this reading odd or even impossible. Allegory nearly always invites hesitation. By using this example we do not seek to recommend Gregory's interpretation; we wish, rather, to illustrate what we hope to show in more detail in chapter 5. Since Gregory assumed that all of scripture somehow aids in the development of the Christian life—a consequence of assuming that the text is the verbal form of divine pedagogy—this particular strategy of reading allowed him to locate his life as a Christian more deeply in seemingly useless passages of the Bible. The vestments of the high priest are to him not just historical curiosities, a kind of textual filler, interesting but irrelevant. For Gregory, they are deeply significant to understanding and living the spiritual life itself. The arrow of analysis does not just move from pomegranate to notions about the philosophical life; it draws those notions into the literal ambiance of scripture. The allegory allows Gregory to attach what he thinks is important (e.g., the spiritual disciplines influential in his own time) to what he knows to be sacred—the literality of scripture.

In addition to discussing the three basic strategies, we hope to explain the larger framework of patristic exegesis. In the next chapter, we describe what is best understood as a substantive patristic theory about the overall meaning of scripture. This theory was not focused on method, nor did it depend upon any particular account of scriptural inspiration and authority. Instead, like modern scientists, the fathers tended to presume rather than articulate the metacritical structure of their investigations. Their focus, also like that of modern scientists, fell on the material body of hypotheses that established the agenda for their tradition of interpretation. As we hope to show, the patristic exegetical project was motivated by a conviction that Jesus of Nazareth is the way, the truth, and the life. Thus, the patristic tradition of interpretation is best understood as a continuous effort to understand how a faith in Jesus Christ brings order and coherence to the disparate data of scripture.

Finally, to complete our analysis of the structure and logic of patristic exegesis, our concluding chapter explains the ways in which the church fathers understood the sources of discipline for exegesis. Neither a theory of meaning, nor a grand hypothesis, nor an array of techniques can establish the difference between good and bad interpretation. As scientists recognize, practices such as peer review encourage good science. Similarly, the fathers recognized that communal accountability was crucial. According to Irenaeus, proper interpretation depends on fidelity to the apostolic witness, preserved in the canonical books and taught by the authority of those bishops who are successors to the apostles. Irenaeus calls this witness the "rule of truth" or "rule of faith." This rule, which over the course of the early centuries of Christianity solidified into creeds, is an interpretive control that directs and orients the exegete as he employs various interpretive techniques.

Unlike most modern intellectuals, the church fathers recognized that good interpretation is most likely to flow from a good person. Patristic exegesis was, finally, a religious exercise. Right reading was a fruit of righteousness. In this way, they affirmed the interpretive form of Aristotle's basic principle: Like seeks like. Insofar as the meaning of scripture directs our attention toward the holiness of God, a reader can only follow and expound that meaning if the soul is purified and prepared to turn its vision toward the divine. "The mind should be cleansed," writes Augustine, "so that it is able to see [divine] light and cling to it once it is seen."[29] The eye of the reader can only follow the scriptures if vision is sanctified.

CHAPTER TWO

Christ Is the End of the Law and the Prophets

Having become man, [Jesus Christ] laid open all the mysteries that had been locked up in Scripture by his Resurrection and Ascension.

JUSTIN MARTYR, *Dialogue with Trypho*

Most contemporary biblical scholars are not, in a strict sense, scholars of the Bible. They are experts who specialize in certain books of the Bible or historical periods in which various portions of it were written. This is naturally so. Our modern historical-critical disciplines focus on discrete portions of scripture, and scholars seek to place the elements of scripture into their historical contexts. Thus, one scholar might pursue research in the Pauline letters, another in the prophetic literature of the Old Testament, and still another might specialize in the body of noncanonical writing such as the Dead Sea Scrolls or the Gnostic gospels. The Bible, as such, is not the object of study; contemporary scholars study aspects of the Bible in their historical contexts.

The specialization of modern study provides insights into the particular contexts and content of the diverse elements of scripture, but it tends to blind us to the basic project of patristic exegesis. No doubt the church fathers had their favorite texts, and they knew some portions of the Bible better than others. However, their goal was to establish an overall interpretation of scripture. The diverse techniques they used to interpret individual passages, their readings of specific episodes and books of scripture, and their adoption of a technical vocabulary in theology were all oriented toward developing a take on the Bible as a whole. For this reason, no matter how diverse the particular exegetical judgments of the church fathers, they were part of a unified interpretive tradition. They could argue over the possibilities of allegorical interpretation. They could offer different interpretations of the first chapters of Genesis. They could use varying terms from the Greek philosophical traditions. All these differences, however, came together under a single goal—to read the Bible as a single text that taught a coherent, unified truth about the nature of God and human destiny.

For the church fathers, the unity of the Bible and the basic commonality of the diverse details of their exegesis, came from the conviction that Jesus Christ is the fulfillment of the law and the prophets. It is natural that they should have adopted this conviction, for the pattern of fulfillment operates within the apostolic writings that were eventually collected and named the New Testament. The church fathers continued and maximized this apostolic effort to develop what we might call a "total reading" of scripture, organized around the fulfilling person of Jesus Christ. We cannot prove that their efforts succeeded. However, we can explain how the fathers pursued this ambitious interpretative project.

The basic structure of the patristic "total reading" of scripture bears some analogies to scientific inquiry. Scientists collect data, and their goal is to find theories that can account for or best interpret the data. The ideal interpretation is the most elegant and comprehensive. For this reason, a general theory of the data, something like a "total reading," serves as a scientific goal. The early Christian exegetical tradition followed this basic pattern. Of course, texts are not the same as experimental data, and the church fathers did not operate according to the same methods as scientists. Nonetheless, the diverse and complex literality of scripture served as a great body of data. They thought it necessary to synthesize this diversity into a single interpretive scheme, and they were convinced that the coming of Jesus as the Messiah or Christ provided them with the basis for formulating a total reading or general theory of scripture. The body of data was fluid around the edges. The canon of scripture was not officially settled until the fourth century, and the fathers never settled on a single way of expressing the unity of scripture. Yet a common project is visible within the diversity. Unified by the conviction that Jesus Christ is the cornerstone of divine truth, the exegesis of the fathers was research into the Christ-centered unity of scripture.[1]

In subsequent chapters, we describe some of the reading strategies that the church fathers used to implement and refine their research project. In this chapter we explain how the general patristic theory of scripture guided their reading of the Bible. First, we need to explain the key claim that animated the patristic interpretive tradition: Jesus Christ is the key to uncovering the real meaning of scripture. Second, we digress into the actual exegetical practice of the church fathers. There is a danger that we might adopt the too simplistic view that Christ *is* himself the general theory of scripture. For the church fathers, to know that Jesus Christ is the incarnate Son of God was the indispensable basis for a total reading. Christ is the light of illumination. However, what they saw as readers needed to be worked out in systematic form. Under pressure from alternative readings of scripture, they needed to identify the shape of the unified interpretation that they believed the revelation of Jesus Christ made possible. Only after we work with a small portion of actual exegesis of scripture, can we turn, finally, to the effort to express the logic of their comprehensive approach to the Bible and explain just how the patristic general theory was put together and applied to the vast scope and diversity of the sacred text.

A Telling Episode

Although no theorist, Ignatius of Antioch was an early Christian leader whose direct style helps us see the central role of convictions about Jesus in patristic exegesis. Ignatius was the bishop of Antioch in Syria, and during a time of persecution he was sent by local authorities to Rome for execution. Those responsible for conveying him to Rome seem to have been lenient, and as he traveled west, Ignatius visited Christian communities in Asia Minor. After leaving these communities, he wrote to clarify and reinforce his teachings. As befits a man on his way to death, Ignatius' letters describe discipleship as following the way of Jesus' suffering and death. In addition, and of more interest to historians of early Christianity who seek to understand the emergence of church structures and systems of governance, Ignatius consistently commended submission to the bishop as the key to maintaining a unified and faithful community.

The forcefulness with which Ignatius insisted upon the authority of the bishop—"We should regard the bishop as the Lord himself"—suggests that his views were not universally accepted.[2] In his letter to the community in Philadelphia, it is quite clear that Ignatius met with resistance. While the specific controversy in that community remains obscure (Ignatius warns broadly of "Judaizing"), there is little uncertainty about his solution. Ignatius insists that the bishop's teaching should determine the matter and unify the community. In saying this, Ignatius is reiterating one of his dominant themes. However, what is unique about his letter to the fractious Philadelphians is that Ignatius steps back for a moment and gives us fleeting insight into the structure and logic of their debate, which turns on scriptural interpretation.

Ignatius' account is cryptic. Against apparent factionalism, Ignatius counsels unity. "Do nothing apart from the bishop," he writes.[3] This teaching, along with exhortations to maintain a holy life in imitation of Jesus, is not presented as optional. He claims to have been taught this fundamental truth by the Spirit, not by "human channels." Just what this distinction between divine and human "channels" means is unclear, but Ignatius' claim to divine authorization for his teaching does not lead him away from scriptural interpretation. The authority of the bishop is part of the prophetic witness, or so Ignatius claims. "Taught by the Spirit" seems to be equivalent to "taught by the scriptures," and the gist of Ignatius' position is that his counsel is fitting because it is the spiritual truth of the sacred texts that all agree must govern communal life.

However much the Philadelphians might agree that the sacred texts are authoritative, they apparently disagree about how to interpret them. By their reading, the authority of the bishop is not an evident truth of scripture. "Where," they ask, "is this taught in the archives?"[4] We can only speculate about the specific documents stored in the communal library, "the archives" of the Philadelphians, but likely they were a collection of sacred texts of Israel—the law, the prophets, and the writings. Whatever the content of the communal library, however, the crux of the issue was exegetical. An influential group of Philadelphians in the Christian community questioned Ignatius' teaching, claiming that he had strayed from the texts and that he was imposing something novel and unwarranted. This raises a key question. What guides right reading of the scriptures? How does one interpret in accord with the Spirit?

Ignatius' response is absolutely crucial for any understanding of patristic exegesis. He acknowledges that some people in Philadelphia doubt his teaching. "When I heard some people saying, 'If I don't find it in the original documents, I don't believe it in the gospel,' I answered them, 'But it is written there.'" This did not satisfy Ignatius' adversaries. "They retorted, 'That's just the question.'" Those who opposed Ignatius' teaching about the authority of bishops were not convinced that he was reading scripture correctly. At this point, Ignatius reveals his fundamental interpretive presupposition. "To my mind it is Jesus Christ who is the original documents. The inviolable archives are his cross and death and his resurrection and the faith that came by him."[5] The conflict of interpretations is blunt. Ignatius' critics find his interpretation strained, an imposition upon the text of something not there. Against them, Ignatius simply insists, "It *is* there," and those who know Jesus Christ will see it. Ignatius does not enter into a discussion of philology, textual detail, or context but pulls out what he takes to be the trump card. Jesus Christ *is* the "original documents." The cross, death, and resurrection of Jesus Christ, and "the faith that came by him," provide the interpretive key. To know him is to know the content of the scriptures.

Ignatius' answer to his critics may strike us as profoundly unsatisfactory. How, we might ask, can he circumvent objections to his interpretation of scripture by appealing to Jesus? What might he mean when he equates Jesus with the scriptures? It is obscure, to say the least, when Ignatius equates a person (Jesus) with a text (the scriptures), and because biblical references are fairly scarce in his letters, we cannot examine his exegetical practice in order to consider his claim. Nonetheless, the central role of Jesus is clear in Ignatius, and it comes to dominate the patristic exegetical tradition. However opaquely, Ignatius expresses the single most defining feature of patristic exegesis: the presumption that knowing the identity of Jesus Christ is the basis for right reading of the sacred writings of the people of Israel.

Making Connections

The early Christian figure who developed arguments to buttress Ignatius' appeal to Jesus as the deciding factor for interpretation was Irenaeus of Lyon. Irenaeus was raised in Asia Minor, and he was a protégé of Polycarp, the bishop of Smyrna, who knew Ignatius. Were we to adopt a developmental, historical approach to patristic exegesis, we would move from Ignatius to Irenaeus. Yet, it is exactly this sequential approach that we wish to avoid. If we draw historical connections between Ignatius and Irenaeus through Polycarp, we can become bewitched by the possibilities of influence and get lost in questions of precedence and development. We can too easily find ourselves describing the trajectory of patristic exegesis rather than analyzing its structure and logic. Therefore, we propose to jump out of the sequence of patristic history and analyze a small portion of exegesis from the hand of Didymus the Blind. This will block the temptation to imagine that we are writing a history of patristic exegesis rather than a historically informed anatomy of that tradition.

Didymus the Blind was a fourth-century exegete who was trained in the Alexandrian school that perpetuated Origen's legacy. That school endorsed its own approaches and emphasized certain allegorical patterns, but we do not turn to Didymus in order to highlight his representation of the uniqueness of the Alexandrian tradition. We are no more interested in differentiating and categorizing strands of patristic exegesis than we are in rewriting a historical account of its development. The difficulty facing contemporary students is not ignorance of the differences between Alexandrian allegory and the more salvation-historical approach of the Asiatic school in which Ignatius and Irenaeus functioned. The main difficulty rests in gaining an understanding of the main interpretive strategies of the church fathers, taken as a whole. Didymus is useful, then, because he can provide us with a small portion of exegesis that exemplifies some of the basic elements of the patristic approach to the Bible.

Didymus provides a patient discussion of Genesis, and his analysis of the first verse of chapter 12 is representative.[6] This verse concerns God's call to Abraham: "Now the lord said to Abram, 'Go from your country and your kindred and your father's house to the land that I will show you.' " Following the tradition of ancient Jewish and Christian interpreters, Didymus presumes that Abraham's father was an idolater. Thus, the literal or narrative sense of the text is straightforward. God seeks to remove Abraham, whom God wishes to favor with the dignity of divine blessing, from the shameful environment of his father's house. Didymus, however, is not satisfied with this level of interpretation, and he immediately makes a general observation about the spiritual life. Evil spirits, he notes, afflict those who are zealous for righteousness, and rightly does God call us out of such situations of temptation. Didymus finds support in the New Testament, pointing out that Jesus taught us that we must hate our brothers and father, sisters and mother, if we are to follow him (Luke 14:26, Matt 16:24). To this he adds the testimony of the disciples, who announce that they have left everything to follow Jesus (Mark 10:28, Matt 19:27). These specific links to the New Testament are framed in terms of the larger divine project. Didymus reads Psalm 45:10–11 ("Hear, O Daughter, consider and incline your ear; forget your people and your father's house, and the King will desire your beauty") as addressed to the church. Constituted by Gentiles who have left their people and the idolatry of their homelands, the church, like Abraham, is being led into a "celestial land." Thus does God turn us away from worldly loyalties controlled by the devil and move us toward heavenly loyalties.

Didymus' interpretive moves are utterly conventional. He follows the lead of

the verbal association of leaving/hating fathers. He establishes a figural connection between Abraham's departure from his father's house and the Gentile
pilgrimage out of the religious practices of their fathers and into the church,
and as he does throughout his commentary, Didymus outlines an allegorical
layering of literal and spiritual. In the coming chapters we explain these exegetical techniques in detail. Nonetheless, even before we analyze the particular
moves he makes, we can use Didymus to refine our understanding of Ignatius'
fundamental principle that Jesus Christ *is* the sacred text.

Didymus certainly does not treat Jesus Christ as the subject matter of Genesis
12:1, at least not in any immediate or obvious sense of *being* the text, as Ignatius
seems to insist. Instead, Didymus connects different scriptural passages according to verbal similarities as well as common patterns. The overall effect is a
densely presented, multifaceted set of exegetical comments that achieves a
striking degree of coherence. Jesus Christ may not *be* this text, but *something*
seems to guide Didymus' interpretive leaps from Genesis to Jesus' teaching, to
the example of the disciples, to Psalm 45. For Didymus, Genesis 12:1 is certainly
about Abraham, but it is also about something—or someone—that overarches
the scriptures as a whole, extending to the spiritual life itself. The way in which
Didymus' reading of Genesis 12:1 has a form or gestalt suggests a link to Ignatius. Jesus may not be the text, but there seems to be an informing, shaping
principle that gives coherence and order to the many details of the text.

Many will correctly point out that as a participant in the Alexandrian school,
Didymus was influenced by the Neoplatonic assumptions of that school. We
might suppose, then, that these influences shape Didymus' exegesis. Clearly,
Neoplatonism is present in Didymus (and in a great deal of the patristic tradition). However, as students of patristic exegesis, we need to distinguish between
the material elements of exegesis such as we find in Didymus' commentary and
its formal structure. The material elements are analogous to the building materials used to construct houses. For our purposes, the key questions do not concern the building materials of patristic exegesis, such as the Neoplatonic philosophical anthropology and cosmology that was so widely influential. The more
important questions are structural. Where is the door located? How is the door
situated in relationship to the stairs and the kitchen? What were the architectural plans?

When we ask these questions of Didymus, attention shifts away from his
Neoplatonic characterization of the spiritual life to the structuring principles of
his exegesis. We think that these principles bear some analogy to mathematical

series and formulas. Numbers are formal entities, and they have the ability to expose and display formal relationships very well. That is why modern science so favors numerical representation. To exploit the explanatory power of numerical representation, we want to briefly digress and illustrate how we normally "interpret" arrangements of numbers. We hope that this digression helps illuminate some of the formal aspects of Didymus' exegesis and, by extension, the patristic tradition as a whole. For although the church fathers did not set out to interpret arrangements of numbers, they did undertake an analogous task: the interpretation of the divinely ordered and arranged words of the Bible.

Consider an ambiguous series of numbers such as "2, 4, . . ." We can interpret that series as $x + 2$. In doing so we are connecting the numerical series to a formula. Most of us do not see this connection as an interpretation. We tend to see $x + 2$ as a handy restatement of the series, but a series is not the same as a formula. The formula $x + 2$ can express a series that might start elsewhere, for example, "102, 104, . . ." For this reason, we can distinguish between a *sequential interpretation* of a series of numbers and *interpretation by formula*. When asked the "meaning" of a series such as "2, 4, . . ." we can make a local comment such as "6, 8, 10." This clarifies the pattern by extending the series. The sequential interpretation offers "6, 8, 10" as an "argument" that the pattern in the series is not "2, 4, 8, 16, . . ." We can make the same point with an interpretation by the formula $x + 2$. When we do this, we are arguing that the series should not be interpreted as x^2.

Let us return to the world of words. Consider a straightforward example of the way in which we often use sequential interpretation and interpretation by formula. The Greek word *logos* has a variety of English translations: word, reason, logic, rationale, and so forth. The church fathers make heavy use of this word, and the variety can make interpretation difficult. To guide their judgment, scholars of early Christianity often use a form of sequential interpretation. They gather a range of uses of *logos* to see if there is a common pattern. This is similar to interpreting a numerical series by extending it: "2, 4, . . ." is interpreted as "2, 4, 6, 8." Once we have enough examples of the use of *logos*, we can settle on a translation.

Some scholars are not satisfied with gathering examples. They use a form of interpretation by formula. This involves two interpretive moves. First, scholars show how Neoplatonism was very influential in patristic thought. With the influence established, scholars then explain how that philosophy has a technical and precise meaning for *logos*. The Neoplatonic meaning can serve, then, as the guide for translating patristic use of *logos*. In other words, Neoplatonic philosophy provides the formula, the $x + 2$, for understanding how the fathers use *logos*. Of course, nearly all scholarly work mixes both approaches. The scholar adduces examples that back up the claim that the Neoplatonic concept of *logos* predominates, or the scholar attempts to sum up the general form of the use of *logos* as found in many instances. Nonetheless, the two approaches are distinct even when applied in tandem.

If we return to Didymus, we find that his exegesis argues in both ways. He highlights episodes such as Abraham's departure from his father's house as described in Genesis 12; Jesus' teaching that his followers must hate brothers, sisters, mothers, and fathers; the willingness of the disciples to sacrifice all for the sake of Jesus as told in the gospels; and the Gentile abandonment of idolatry in the centuries of the growth of Christianity. These four elements—three biblical texts and the pattern of cultural change effected by Christianity—function as a series in Didymus' exegesis. They are a sequential interpretation in the same way that adding "6, 8, 10" to a series such as "2, 4, . . ." clarifies and extends the "meaning." The discrete instances build up and reinforce a formal pattern.

Into this series Didymus interpolates more general remarks. He suggests that all four elements have a common pattern of leaving for the sake of righteousness. He calls this pattern the spiritual meaning. The notion that one of the basic features of the spiritual life involves turning away from worldly preoccupation in search of heavenly truths is common among the church fathers, and it is definitive of the Alexandrian school in which Didymus functioned. Again, the point is not where he got the idea. What matters is how it is used. In the exegesis, the pattern seems to function as a formula. Of course, the notion of leaving or turning from worldly pursuits (idolatry) toward the heavenly (righteousness) is not as precise as a mathematical formula. Nonetheless, it does function as the $x + 2$ of his four elements. The interpretation by formula allows him to range across highly diverse material and draw together the particular elements into a single, sustained series of exegetical comments.

We need to avoid overinterpreting Didymus' interpretation. Didymus does not try to force the heterogeneous text of Genesis into a single pattern of turning away from worldliness and toward heavenly truth. His exegesis is more loosely developed; he describes the pattern but it is not superimposed or drawn out as a conclusion. Nor should we assume, as do many modern readers of the Alexandrian tradition of exegesis, that the pattern or formula is somehow prior to or more fundamental than the extensive displays of specific sequences of texts that actually constitute the bulk of Didymus' (and all patristic) interpretation. His exegesis is not, in a word, formulaic. Like Gregory's exegesis of the rods and serpents in Exodus 7, Didymus finds and expounds patterns, but he does not move out of the literal ambiance of scripture. Even as he uses the spiritual pattern of turning from the worldly toward the heavenly, Didymus remains tied to the verbal sequences within the text.

Didymus uses sequential interpretation and interpretation by formula to develop a larger, unified reading of Genesis. He makes connections and follows textual hints according to what we might call a comprehensive interpretation. To show this global interpretation at work would require us to undertake a large-scale exposition of Didymus' exegesis. This is a daunting prospect, for just as the local interpretation of Genesis 12:1 draws on sequence and formula, Didymus' comprehensive interpretation rests on an extended, largely implicit understanding of the sequence of events that stretch from the creation of the world through the Word to its consummation in Christ, as well as on a formula shaped by the Alexandrian Christology that Didymus inherited and presumes. Instead of undertaking such a task, we turn to Irenaeus of Lyons. Like Ignatius, Irenaeus was forced by controversy to say something about how to read rightly. Unlike Ignatius, he responded to his adversaries with a fully drawn theory of how to read the Bible as a unified whole. Didymus, like nearly all the church fathers, presupposed this general theory of scripture in his approach to the many details of the Bible.

A General Theory of Patristic Interpretation

A Greek-speaking Christian born around 140, Irenaeus migrated west to the Roman province of Gaul and served the church as a teacher, presbyter, and eventually bishop. It was in Gaul, in the city of Lyons, that Irenaeus confronted a tradition of spiritual teaching promulgated by the Valentinians, named for Valentinus, a teacher who flourished in Rome in the second century. Just what the Valentinians taught is complex and obscured by the fact that our primary source of information is Irenaeus' extensive attack upon this teaching in his treatise *On the Detection and Refutation of Knowledge Falsely So Called* or, according to its more popular title, *Against the Heresies*. Nonetheless, we can be quite certain why Irenaeus thought the Valentinian teachers needed to be resisted. They were not just false teachers. Irenaeus' world was full of competing philosophies and religions. The Valentinians were heretics in Irenaeus' eyes because they claimed that their teachings were the true and accurate interpretation of the sacred texts of the church. As Irenaeus reports, "These men falsify the oracles of God and prove themselves evil interpreters of the good word of revelation."[7] The root of the controversy was exegesis.

For Irenaeus to succeed in his goal of refuting such teaching, he needed to explain just how and why the Valentinians interpreted falsely. Irenaeus had to show how he, the representative of true teaching, read the scriptures rightly. To a very great extent, he makes the case against his adversaries detail by detail. He shows the absurdity of Valentinian teaching and how it comes from disreputable sources. He insinuates that it is associated with immoral behavior. But most of all, Irenaeus pursues countless exegetical arguments and subarguments. These interpretive arguments are often similar in form to the small portion of Didymus' exegesis of Genesis that we have analyzed. Irenaeus develops what he takes to be a plausible series of textual elements, sometimes in the mode of what we are calling a sequential interpretation and at other times in the mode of interpretation by formula. He then juxtaposes them to what he takes to be disordered heretical readings. However, at various points in *Against the Heresies,* Irenaeus steps back from his work of refutation and, drawing on the technical vocabulary of classical rhetoric, offers broader observations about the difference between true and false interpretation.[8] Among these, Irenaeus provides a sketch of what proved to be the dominant patristic theory of the unified truth of scripture. It is an approach that vindicates Ignatius' assertion that Jesus Christ is the sacred text and provides us with insight into the structuring principles that guided the interpretation of other patristic figures such as Didymus. To develop his theory, Irenaeus borrows three key terms from classical rhetoric. They are *hypothesis, economy,* and *recapitulation.*[9] All three help Irenaeus explain how his own approach, which he insists is the orthodox tradition of interpretation, establishes the broadest meaning of scripture, while the heretical readers, he argues, dismember the text by reading it against the grain of its larger sense.

Irenaeus' use of *hypothesis* is clearest and closest to our modern assumptions about interpretation. We have already seen examples of the concept of hypothesis at work. To venture the suggestion of "6, 8, 10" or $x + 2$ is to offer a hypothesis about the meaning of "2, 4, . . ." Irenaeus, however, uses hypothesis in a more strictly literary sense. In the ancient rhetorical tradition, the gist of a literary work was called its hypothesis.[10] In our time, we restrict the concept of hypothesis to scientific matters. For us the term has more abstract overtones than it had for the ancients. Nevertheless, with the differences duly noted, the basic notion that a literary work has a hypothesis remains. For example, after seeing Arthur Miller's play *The Crucible,* we might argue about its meaning or hypothesis. This argument concerns the play taken as a whole. Does the play hold together best when seen as a warning against the dangers of McCarthyism, or is that hypothesis too limiting? Perhaps *The Crucible* is best understood as a parable about our fears of the unknown and the ways in which the unscrupulous can play upon those fears. In any event, the larger meaning or hypothesis of the play remains open, and arguing for one position or another is the stuff of college essays. The important point is that literary works such as *The Crucible* positively invite reflection on the hypothesis.

For Irenaeus, the key failure of heretical interpretation is that it does not identify the hypothesis of the Bible. It picks up details, exploits local correspondences, manipulates symbols, but in the end such a reading does not show how the beginning, middle, and end hang together. At one point Irenaeus uses the analogy of a mosaic to make his point about the interpretive failure of the Valentinians. Their interpretations read "as if someone destroyed the figure of a man in the authentic portrait of a king, carefully created by a skillful artist out of precious stones, and rearranged the stones to make the image of a dog or fox, declaring that this badly composed image is that good image of the king made by the skillful artist." The heretical readers do not ignore scripture but use it to compose a distorted picture. According to Irenaeus, they make the individual pieces of the mosaic of scripture "into the image of a dog, and by the appearance of the stones deceives the simple, that is, those ignorant of the king's image, and persuades them that this ugly image of the fox is the good image of the king."[11] The simple are led astray because the blue tiles remain blue. The ability of the false readers to use a verse here and a verse there gives plausibility to their false image of the whole.

In this analogy, the role of a hypothesis becomes clear. When one reads the Bible, there are details that require analysis. One needs to know the color of the tile, and this may require answering local questions. To recall Didymus' comments on Genesis 12:1, one may need to think about why Abraham had to leave his father's house, and one may need to compare this local "color" with other "pieces." Didymus does this by establishing his sequences and outlining a spiritual formula. However, the greater task is to see the place of all the pieces in a larger picture, to see the hypothesis by which the individual verses or portions of the Bible fit together with all the rest. In short, to read rightly, one needs to know the overall plan. Faced with inconclusive or fragmentary evidence, one needs to know the hypothesis that will give the proper ordering and guide understanding. The key to Irenaeus' polemic against those whom he thinks false teachers is that their reading of scripture is guided by the wrong overall judgment about the gist of the scriptural text. Their hypothesis, he argues, is a deformed image constructed according to implausible cosmological theories, numerological schemes, and arbitrary use of scriptural language.

We do not want to discuss whether or not Irenaeus correctly assessed the exegesis of his adversaries. We prefer to focus on understanding how Irenaeus uses the notion of hypothesis. He provides another helpful analogy. Irenaeus imagines an assembly of verses from Homer that a clever reader might construct.[12] This clever reader takes a verse here and a verse there out of the *Iliad* and *Odyssey*. The goal is not to summarize the basic plot of either. Instead, the clever reader rearranges the verses to exploit certain names and images. In the illustration Irenaeus provides, the rearrangement of the verses yields a lament about Hercules rather than an epic about Achilles and Odysseus. Homer's raw material is used to construct a poem based upon an alien hypothesis that is false to the thrust or hypothesis of the Homeric epics from which the verses are taken.

According to Irenaeus, the false teachers are doing the same thing with the verses of scripture. They make reference to Adam and Eve, Abraham, Moses, and Jesus, but they do so according to an alien hypothesis. Seeking to teach spiritual truths, these sages try to arrange the details of the biblical narrative according to a scheme of epochs and emanations that reflects their vision of redemption. In other words, unable to make sense of why Abraham or Moses or Joshua or Jesus might matter as events presented in the sequence one finds in the Old and New Testaments, these teachers take scriptural details out of the narrative sequence and reposition them in a new setting, defined by their own hypothesis about the nature of creation and salvation.

Once Irenaeus has identified the problem in heretical exegesis—that its writers are working with a wrongheaded hypothesis—he turns to articulate what he takes to be scripture's proper hypothesis. Irenaeus' analysis is dense, and unlike modern theologians, he does not clearly separate his larger remarks about the logic of the hypothesis of scripture from his many digressions into specific points of controversy. Nonetheless, we can see that Irenaeus explains the plan of the mosaic, the image of the handsome king, in two ways. As Irenaeus writes, in what can be taken as a synopsis of his argument, "There is thus only one God, the Father, as we have shown, and one Jesus Christ our Lord, who came according to the economy and who recapitulated all things in himself."[13] The first crucial term is *economy*. The second is *recapitulation*. Using these two technical concepts, Irenaeus is able to expound the ways in which the ruling hypothesis for orthodox interpretation—that Jesus Christ is the fulfillment of all things—can be applied to the details of scripture.

The word *economy* expresses a concept central to patristic theology. We return to it in each of our subsequent chapters, so we need to be very clear about what it means. It is unfortunately a word that the contemporary mind inevitably associates with the complex forces that drive commerce. The ancient Greek use is more commonsensical and the application is much broader. *Oikonomia* denotes good order and arrangement of affairs. Economy can refer to the well-run household, as well as a well-constructed story. Ancient teachers of rhetoric, much like contemporary teachers of composition, urged careful sequencing of events in historical narratives. A story should have an economy, a structure or plot that allows us to discern the flow of the narrative. The same holds for the arrangement of arguments in speeches or treatises. An outline for a paper or the table of contents for a book provides an economy.

The sense of economy as good order and arrangement is crucial for Irenaeus; the correct hypothesis of scripture must express its economy. His charge is that his adversaries are tearing pieces from their proper places within the mosaic, the larger economy. They are using their false hypothesis to rearrange the details of scripture into a false economy, a false order, just as the clever reader puts verses from Homer into a false sequence. The true and accurate reading of scripture, he argues, must follow the divine economy by which God has put together the mosaic of scripture. There is a good order and arrangement of scripture (and, for Irenaeus, all aspects of creations) that portrays the handsome king.

For Irenaeus, the divine economy is clearly taught by the church. He insists that a proper interpretation of scripture must both presume and discern the sequences of events that are ordained by God. "We hold fast," he writes, "to the rule of truth, that there is one almighty God who founded everything through his Word and arranged it and made everything out of the non-existent."[14] This divinely arranged economy is necessary for understanding any event or episode in the scriptures. One should not attempt to wrench episodes out of this economy. We can only know the meaning of "8" if we see its place in the sequence "2, 4, 6, 8." We can only know how to interpret the account of Noah and his ark if we place it within a divine order of events that stretches from the fall of Adam and Eve, through the election of Abraham, the exodus of the Israelites, the reign of King David, the Babylonian exile, to the coming of Jesus Christ and his fulfillment of all things.

Throughout his treatise, Irenaeus outlines the sequences or economy of scripture that he takes to be indispensable for apostolic teaching. The great teachers of the church, he reports in a typical passage, proclaim "the one God, omnipotent, the maker of heaven and earth, the creator of man, who brought the deluge, and called Abraham, who led the people from the land of Egypt, spoke with Moses, set forth the law, sent the prophets, and who has prepared fire for the devil and his angels."[15] This economy is the sacred outline or table of contents of scripture. The divine economy is the detailed plan by which all the pieces of the mosaic have been placed by God to bring us to see the image of the handsome king. Therefore, this arrangement of world history, this economy, should guide interpretation of scripture. If we follow the divinely coded sequence, then we can properly assess each piece of the mosaic, each moment of biblical history, according to its role in the good order and arrangement ordained by God.

For Irenaeus, the coming of Jesus Christ is the decisive event that clarifies the divine economy. The scriptures anticipate future events. They lay out a sequence or order of divine purpose, but that purpose is unclear. How are the promises to Abraham to be fulfilled? To whom and for how long do the laws delivered to Moses on Mount Sinai apply? Did the prophets foretell a worldly or heavenly kingdom? Will God deliver his people from worldly oppression or the dominion of the devil? Is salvation for the Jews or for all the nations? These are all questions about the divine economy, and without Christ, the economy of God would be as difficult to determine as the series "2, 4, . . ." We would not know whether the series should be continued "2, 4, 6, 8, . . ." or "2, 4, 8, 16, . . ." The coming of Christ, then, functions like the number "6." It clarifies the meaning of the scriptural sequences in the Old Testament. The promise to Abraham is fulfilled in Christ. Christ brings to an end the ritual laws of Israel. The kingdom he establishes is spiritual. He triumphs over sin and death rather than worldly powers. Salvation is for both Jew and Gentile, and so forth. In each instance, the meaning of the prior sequence of divine events is made clear.

For Irenaeus and the patristic tradition, Jesus Christ is more than the indispensable piece of data. He also embodies the "formula" of the series. Thus Irenaeus draws upon recapitulation, another term from the ancient tradition of rhetoric. The patristic tradition does not use Irenaeus' technical term as extensively as it uses the term *economy*. However, the underlying concept is always present in the fathers' exegesis. *Recapitulation* is an English form of *recapitulans,* the Latin translation of *anakephalaiosis,* which means final repetition, summing up, drawing to conclusion. As a term in rhetoric, it refers to the end of a speech, when the speaker drives home the point with a summary of the strongest arguments.

Irenaeus takes over this classical use of recapitulation and adds layers of historical and ontological meaning. Jesus Christ is not only the Father's "summary statement." Christ is the Logos of the Father, the logic or purpose in and through which the whole divine economy is conceived and implemented. Therefore, the coming of the Logos in the man Jesus of Nazareth incarnates and manifests the very purpose of the economy of God. Irenaeus works this out in countless specific instances. For example, the opening chapters of Genesis set into motion events that would seem to undermine the goodness of creation, to be followed by an inconclusive series of covenants that restrain sin but do not restore the original integrity of righteousness. Yet, as Irenaeus argues, even in their incompleteness, each moment in the divine economy anticipates the coming of the Logos incarnate in Jesus Christ. He enters into the drama of fall and covenant, bringing it to completion by defeating the power of sin. Writing of Christ, Irenaeus asserts, "He has therefore, in his work of recapitulation, summed up all things, both waging war against our enemy, and crushing him who had at the beginning led us away captives in Adam."[16] God's final and conclusive argument comes at the end, pulling together the logic and purpose of everything that had been divinely ordained beforehand.

The recapitulation of all things in Jesus Christ, for Irenaeus, is not an arbitrary ending. It is not the assertion of a "6" that determines our reading of a series such as "2, 4, . . ." that could be completed differently. It cannot be arbitrary because Jesus Christ is the incarnate divine Logos. However, Irenaeus does not rest with dogmatic assertion. He instead undertakes an exegetical demonstration of the true fulfillment of all things in Christ. He shows in countless digressions into the details of biblical history that Jesus Christ is the key to all the inconclusive patterns and open questions raised by scripture. He is the "*x* + 2." Adam does not fall in an abstract sense. His disobedience comes from the fruit of the tree, and from that tree comes death. Jesus Christ recapitulates this scene, though now in the key of righteousness rather than sin. Christ's obedience triumphs over sin by his death upon the tree of the cross, and the fruit of that tree is life. Or again, just as occasion for sin comes from a woman (Eve), so does the possibility of righteousness come from a woman (the Virgin Mary). Or again, just as the fall was the greatest victory of the devil, the cross of Christ was his greatest defeat.[17] All the details fit, argues Irenaeus, if only we assume that Jesus Christ is the incarnate Word of God.

Our goal is not to present Irenaeus' exegetical arguments in detail. We simply wish to provide some clarity about how Irenaeus thought a faith in Jesus Christ as the Son of God functions as the singular key, the hypothesis for Christian exegesis. In a long passage, Irenaeus indicates that faith in Jesus Christ provides the crucial basis for interpreting countless scriptural and theological puzzles. If we take Jesus Christ as the hypothesis, the structuring principle for the project of ordering the vast mosaic of scripture, then we

> may bring out the meaning of those things which have been spoken in parables, and accommodate them to the general scheme of the faith; and explain the operation and economy of God connected with human salvation; and show that God manifested compassion in regard to the apostasy of the angels who transgressed, as also with respect to the disobedience of men; and set forth why it is that one and the same God has made some things temporal and some eternal, some heavenly and others earthly; and understand for what reason God, though invisible, manifested himself to the prophets, not under one form, but differently to different individuals; and show why it was that more covenants than one were given to mankind; and teach what was the special character of these covenants; and search out for what reason "God hath concluded every man in unbelief that he may have mercy on all" (Rom 11:32); and gratefully describe on what account the Word of God become flesh and suffered; and relate why the advent of the Son of God took place in these last times, that is, in the end, rather than in the beginning; and unfold what is contained in the Scriptures concerning the end, and things to come; and not to be silent as to how it is that God has made the Gentiles, whose salvation was despaired of, fellow-heirs, and of the same body, and partakers with the saints; and discourse on how it is that "this mortal body shall put on immortality, and this corruptible shall put on incorruption" (1 Corinthians 15:54).[18]

For Irenaeus, then, the interpretive value of faith in Jesus Christ is huge. To believe in Jesus Christ as the Son of the one God, who is creator of heaven and earth, allows for an account of any number of interpretive difficulties, not only problems internal to the divine economy (e.g., why the old covenant is different from the new covenant) but also theological problems of the most basic sort (e.g., how it could befit the dignity of God to become flesh and suffer). Christ is the "$x + 2$" who provides the basis for a comprehensive interpretation.

Thus, Irenaeus explains Ignatius' enigmatic claim that Jesus Christ *is* the sacred text. As Irenaeus observes, to presume that Jesus Christ is the Son of God allows the reader of scripture to affirm a God "who does not use violent means to obtain what he desires; so that neither should justice be infringed upon, nor the ancient handiwork of God go to destruction."[19] Such a hypothesis allows us to read the text as teaching an economy that is well sequenced rather than disordered. To shift from our analogy of numerical order to that of architectural structure, for Irenaeus, placing Jesus Christ as the cornerstone allows one to read the scriptures as a well-constructed edifice rather than treating it as a quarry from which to draw individual stones to be laid according to some other scheme. As Irenaeus writes, "Every prophecy, before its fulfillment is to man [full of] enigmas and ambiguities. But when the time has arrived, and the prediction has come to pass, then the prophecies have a clear and certain exposition." Appealing to one of Jesus' parables, for Irenaeus, the discrete portions of scripture are as "a treasure, hid indeed in a field, but brought to light by the cross of Christ, both enriching the understanding of men, and showing forth the wisdom of God, and declaring his economy with regard to man."[20] Jesus Christ is not the Bible. The scriptures remain the vast body of heterogeneous material, retaining its reality as a text that speaks about a vast array of events and people, and records laws, parables, proverbs, prayer, and poems. However, for Irenaeus and the patristic tradition as a whole, Jesus Christ is the hypothesis. He reveals the logic and architecture by which a total reading of that great diversity and literal reality may be confidently pursued.

How the patristic hypothesis of Jesus Christ as the recapitulation of the economy of salvation exercised its comprehensive ambition can be seen in the great early Christian project of rereading the scriptures that the church inherited from Judaism. Justin Martyr was a second-century student of Greek philosophy who became a follower of Christ. In addition to writing treatises to show how faith in Christ satisfied the aspirations of Greek philosophy, he wrote the *Dialogue with Trypho* to demonstrate that faith in Christ unraveled all the interpretive puzzles of the Old Testament. In the *Dialogue,* Trypho is a Jew, and against him the voice of Justin is one of interpretive confidence, even aggression. The topic of discussion, says Justin, is "your books, or should I say, ours: for we are the ones who follow their line of thought."[21] Justin claims to know the scheme by which the mosaic of scripture can be interpreted so that it makes visible the image of the handsome king. Without this hypothesis, the pieces are mishandled. "Nobody," Justin writes with confidence, "will be able to receive Abraham's heritage, except those whose way of thinking is in utter conformity with the faith of Abraham through the acknowledgement of all the mysteries."[22] The mysteries are, of course, those revealed in Christ. The mysteries of Christ are the crucial key to proper interpretation. Christ guides the reader toward the true argument, the true logic of scripture, and for this reason, Justin is confident that he, and not Trypho the Jew, is the rightful interpreter of the law and the prophets. Like Irenaeus against his heretical opponents, Justin asserts that he knows the governing hypothesis. This conviction that Christ fulfilled and clarified the scriptures animated the entire patristic exegetical project.[23]

Our goal is not to *prove* that the patristic tradition is correct. That would entail undertaking a massive project of reading the entire scriptural story, from Genesis to Revelation, as a coherent whole that not only accords with our assumptions about particular passages in scripture but also conforms to our assumptions about the nature of God, history, and salvation. It would require us to reproduce the entire body of patristic exegesis—and do so in an idiom that properly addresses the objections and difficulties of our own age. Our goal is much more modest. We simply seek to show patristic exegetical assumptions and to clarify their general theory of interpretation. Here, there can be little doubt. The church fathers were convinced that Jesus Christ shed light on all things and provided the basis for the true reading of scripture. Hilary of Poitiers perhaps expressed best this ancient conviction at the beginning of his *Treatise on the Mysteries:*

> Every work contained in the sacred books announces with words, reveals by the facts, and establishes by example the coming of our Lord Jesus Christ who, sent by his father, became a man, being born of a virgin by the work of the Holy Spirit. It is, therefore, he who, throughout this present age engenders, washes, sanctifies, chooses, separates out, and redeems the church in the true and manifest figures of the Patriarchs: by the sleep of Adam, by the flood of Noah, by the blessing of Melchizedek, by the justification of Abraham, by the birth of Isaac, and by the servitude of Jacob. Through the entire unfolding of time, in a word, the assembly of the prophets, serving the divine economy, gave us knowledge of his coming incarnation.[24]

Every aspect of scripture leans toward Christ, and to know his coming is like discovering the crucial piece of evidence or overarching hypothesis that suddenly brings the whole array of data into focus.

Saying does not make it so. Hilary (and Ignatius, Didymus, Irenaeus, and the rest of the patristic interpreters) may claim that the entire sweep of scripture can be interpreted in and through the person of Jesus Christ, but the great bulk of patristic exegesis does not *say* this directly. Throughout this chapter we have exercised ourselves to find the moments in patristic treatises where the church fathers make summary or general statements about their interpretive project. These moments are infrequent because nearly all patristic writing is a cumulative effort to *show* the hypothesis of Christ at work in the details of exegesis. This huge effort of showing the interpretive power of Christ is one reason that their treatises, even when addressing doctrinal topics, are so saturated with the details of scripture. The fathers gathered up the endless tiny pieces of the scriptural mosaic. As they did so, they did not mechanically apply Christ as a formula. For the church fathers read in order not only to apply the truth of God in Jesus Christ and in so doing clarify the meaning of scripture, but also to gain knowledge of him through his illuminating power.

For this reason, the fathers were not dogmatists. They were extraordinarily ambitious, and as we have seen in Irenaeus and Justin, they were confident that they had the correct approach to scripture. However, their confidence did not translate into negligence or arrogance. They did not read scripture to prove their doctrines, and they did not use their doctrines to wrest scripture out of the hands of those they thought heretics. The notion that the church fathers were smug and complacent, using their doctrinal commitments to oppress open-minded and liberal adversaries, is a lamentable anachronism.

In the first place, to adopt a general theory for the interpretation of scripture, as did the fathers in their affirmation of Jesus Christ as the hypothesis of scripture, was to embark on an excruciatingly difficult, indeed, impossible project—to seek a total or comprehensive interpretation of the Bible. This comprehensive reading could not be asserted any more than a comprehensive account of Milton's *Paradise Lost* can simply be stated in the form of a hypothesis. Interpreters must make their cases line by line, book by book. The material must be analyzed, organized, and brought into just the right order according to the economy that the interpreter thinks best captures the ebb and flow of text. For this reason, the exegesis of scripture was, for the fathers, an unending process of close examination and reexamination of the details. Their confidence that Jesus Christ was the hypothesis of scripture did not translate into a complacent assumption that they possessed a true and final understanding.

More importantly, Irenaeus may have adopted the analogy of the mosaic, but he knew that the image of the handsome king, in the case of scripture, is a heavenly one that the human mind cannot comprehend. Exegesis, for the fathers, was not an academic exercise to be undertaken in order to prove already held beliefs. Exegesis was a spiritual discipline, a journey through the literality of scripture in which one is not only to dwell in the clear teachings of Jesus or the great theological pronouncements of Paul but by the very ambition of a total reading of scripture one is led through the thickets and brambles of seeming contradiction, blank oceans and dry deserts of obscure and uncertain material. For the fathers did not hold Jesus Christ as an inert truth; they believed that they could only dwell in him, and he in them, if they dwelled in his illuminating light. To read under his guidance was to dwell in his light; to interpret the mosaic of scripture was to catch a glimpse of his image.

CHAPTER THREE

Intensive Reading

We shall walk more safely by the aid of the scriptures themselves

AUGUSTINE, *On Christian Doctrine*

Crossword puzzles have themes such as film noir, the 1950s, and so forth. To know the theme is to have a broad clue about how to work out the specific words in the puzzle. Yet this broad clue no more relieves one of the task of working with the particular hints and piecing together the puzzle word by word than Irenaeus' articulation of the divine economy distracted him from an interpretation of the scriptures that must be undertaken episode by episode, word by word. For the church fathers, a faith that Jesus Christ fulfills the scriptures did not supersede or make unnecessary the difficult task of struggling with the literal details of the Bible. Quite the contrary, the task of exegesis was central, and the hypothesis of Christ gave just the right focus to the highly particular, intensive work of reading the details of scripture so that they fit together into an interlocking whole.

Exploring countless scriptural details with an eye toward assembling a full and complete picture marks the most basic "method" of patristic exegesis. To recall Irenaeus' image of a mosaic, the church fathers worked hard to identify the color, shape, and texture of each small piece of scripture, always thinking about the place of each element in the overarching figure of the handsome king. By paying close attention to the words of scripture, early Christian readers sought to achieve their ambition: to achieve a "total reading" of the Bible. Thus, the overall reading was not developed in broad strokes or with large abstractions; it was carefully constructed verse by verse. In this sense, for all the ambition of patristic biblical interpretation, the church fathers were intensive readers ever on the lookout for hints and signs amid the tiniest details of the text.

To a great extent, attention to detail is a self-evident point of departure for the work of interpreting texts, whether sacred or secular, ancient, medieval, or modern, and a good reader is nearly always an intensive reader. Interpreting requires us to make sense of what is written, and the letters, words, and sentences are the building blocks of whatever we might take to be the larger meaning. We read along in a book and come upon an unfamiliar word. If we cannot puzzle out the meaning on our own, we reach for a dictionary. If the word comes at a key juncture in the passage, then interpreting the word—deciding what it means—is integral to the larger goal of interpreting. Sometimes the actual marks on the page can be puzzling. Handwritten texts are notorious for providing moments of frustration as we try to make out just which letters are which. Here, no dictionary can save the day. We need to puzzle out a plausible reading, subtly moving from the marks on the page to our mental picture of what would make sense in the larger context of the sentence.

These problems were common in the ancient world. Ancient texts were written without capitalization and punctuation, so an interpreter first had to organize the words into sentences. Moreover, in an era long before the invention of the printing press, texts had to be copied by hand in order to be reproduced and circulated. Errors inevitably crept into widely read works. A word would fall out here and there, and in other places, words would be added or altered. Again, a close reader needs to be on guard against such errors and correct them as best he can by consulting other manuscripts and comparing them. In all these instances, concrete literal interpretive difficulties emerged for the church fathers.[1]

Words on the page can challenge in more complex ways that transcend the particular limitations of ancient approaches to writing and publication. Consider, for example, the great twentieth-century philosopher, Martin Heidegger, notorious for his idiosyncratic formulations and almost occult use of language. A key term in his philosophy is *being-there*. When reading Heidegger, a dictionary will not help. Instead, we must hold in our minds some of the many passages in which Heidegger uses the term and, in this way, build up a larger sense of context. Knowing that Heidegger wrote in German we can consult the original in hopes that the German term *Dasein* will shed some light. Should we still be baffled, we can consult a philosophy professor who attended Heidegger's lectures, or who was a student of someone who attended his lectures, and by way of relying on the authority of an individual who has a more intimate acquaintance with the atmosphere of the text, clarify the meaning of Heidegger's term.

From dictionaries to comparing manuscripts, from researching original languages to consulting experts, we call these *lexical* strategies for reading. The church fathers consistently sought lexical strategies to find a reasonable basis for assigning reliable meanings to key words and elements in texts. Sometimes, however, authors do not use strange or unfamiliar words. Instead, they use familiar words strangely, by saying something that seems unlikely or even seemingly contradictory. For example, the seventeenth-century mathematician, philosopher, and Christian apologist Blaise Pascal wrote, "The heart has its reasons that reason cannot know." The verbal juxtaposition forces thought. How can there be *reasons* that are beyond the ken of *reason*? To answer this question may require us to use lexical strategies. How does Pascal use words such as *heart* and *reason* in other passages? What was the standard use in the seventeenth century? Whatever the results of such research, the apparent contradiction creates a tension that demands interpretation. Our lexical inquiries must return to the puzzle of reasons unknown by reason.

Thus, to the lexical strategies of interpretation we add a *dialectical* strategy of reading, an approach that considers two seemingly contradictory or incongruous elements of a text. It is crucial to see that intensive readers do not wait to be struck across the head with patent contradiction. They press and test, searching out potential implausibilities, seeming contradictions and paradoxes, as well as apparent misuses of language. We call this strategy dialectical because it recognizes that the single voice of the text often divides into two (or perhaps more) voices that speak against each other rather than as one. In Pascal's case, there would seem to be reasons outside of reason, and this is surely a difficulty to be solved. In fact, we can be fairly sure that Pascal deliberately formulated the paradox in order to force his readers to rethink just what the word *reason* might mean.

The goal of the dialectical strategy is not to undermine or deconstruct the text, anymore than Pascal sought to corrupt or destroy our confidence in reason. Rather, the dialectical strategy challenges our assumption that the unified surface of the text is sufficient and presses for a deeper coherence. Following hints in the text that suggest problems, incoherences, even inconsistencies, this strategy of interpretation forces the intensive reader to become articulate about just how a text that seems divided against itself is, in fact, of one mind. Or to express the dialectical strategy slightly differently, by suggesting why we might think a text says something false, a degree of interpretive tension is created that presses us to clarify just how the text is saying something true. For this reason, dialectical reading is a heroic strategy that tests and deepens interpretation by finding problems and challenges for the reader. The key point, however, is that the problems and challenges come from within the text, not from quite interesting and legitimate questions that readers might ask from outside. The puzzle is what Pascal means when he says that there are reasons unknown by reason, not why he came to believe, as he did, in a severe, Jansenist form of Roman Catholicism.

In addition to the lexical and dialectical strategies of intensive reading, we add a third, more fluid and wide-ranging strategy, which we call the *associative* strategy. The associative strategy involves the countless ways in which particular words, images, or phrases are joined together in our minds. In a certain sense, the lexical and dialectical strategies are associative. For a dictionary provides definitions by associating a word with synonyms or descriptions, and the dialectical strategy probes unlikely or improbable associations that beg for explanation. There are, however, more open-ended forms of association, such as meter, alliteration, and rhyme. The human mind relishes verbal patterns: "Peter Piper picked a pepper . . ." While the ability to find them in texts may be undervalued in our scientific age (which is enamored of numerical patterns rather than word patterns), in antiquity, identifying such patterns was often viewed as a sign that a reader was on the right path. Our own time may not be as far removed from this poetic sensibility as we imagine. One feature of postmodern literary theory is a love of cute titles and clever terminology, and this love echoes the ancient presumption that finding and exposing verbal patterns is a key element of interpretation. A feminist literary critic who titles an essay "The Reproduction of Othering" is exploiting a range of associations that connects a key notion in postmodern philosophy (alterity or "otherness") with a basic assumption of postmodern literary theory (that literature is a form of cultural production) and a feminist theme (fertility). On a more mundane level, a well-wrought pun brings a smile, and many chuckle when they hear a clever limerick. In both instances, what tickles the fancy is the play of words, not just the content of the sentence.

Mere play is not sufficient in most cases. An alliterative association of adjectives appeals because the underlying meanings of the words make sense. Thus, a broader associative strategy of interpretation involves exploring a potentially unlimited range of connections that turn not only on the literality of words but also their capacity to evoke layers of meaning. Almost any poem could illustrate. Consider, for example, "Elegy Written in a Country Church-Yard," written by the eighteenth-century English poet Thomas Gray. The first stanza calls to mind the day's end: "The Curfew tolls the knell of parting day." A few stanzas later, Gray evokes images of the graves where "the rude Forefathers of the hamlet sleep." Still further on in the poem, the images shift to evoke the dignity of the rural lives buried in the graveyard, "Far from the madding crowd's ignoble strife." These elements—day's end, the silent graves, the dignity of rural life—are only pieces of a complex poem. However, our minds easily associate the first stanza's image of the day's end with the passing from life to death, memorialized by the gravestones. The three quoted lines seem to belong together as evocations of endings. Further, we can make a more adventurous link, associating the day's end and gravestones with the passing of premodern, rural forms of life in the early days of the Industrial Revolution. The day does not last forever; human life is not eternal; the culture we cherish will also be eclipsed. Thus, the interpretation moves from fading light, to fading life, to a fading social system.

What do such associations achieve? It is difficult to say just how and why the human mind is capable of responding so synthetically to the use of words. It seems almost second nature for a reader to move from word to word, image to image, and in so doing construct an interpretation that does not "explain" the text, but rather illuminates or organizes it. Just as the words of a crossword puzzle cross and, in crossing, provide decisive clues about what comes next, so the words and images of texts cross and lead the reader forward toward the construction of associations only latent and potential in the material at hand. This building up of crossing links is the basic goal of the associative strategy.

With these three strategies in mind, we turn to some specific examples in the church fathers' work. Like any sophisticated interpretive tradition, patristic exegesis involves a complex use of many different exegetical strategies. The fathers combine the lexical, dialectical, and associative with ease, and these moves are often part of their efforts to develop typological and allegorical readings. This can make their exegesis difficult to isolate into a single strategy for explication. Furthermore, modern readers use different lexical aids than did the church fathers. We are satisfied by different dialectical solutions to difficult passages and attracted to other forms of association. Nonetheless, we are convinced that the basic strategies are intelligible, even commonplace in our own time. Our hope is that these illustrations clarify just how the church fathers focused their minds on the particularity of scripture. With some clarity about these strategies, we can understand how early Christian interpreters shaped their intensive reading.

Lexical Strategies

The scriptures of Israel were written in an ancient form of Hebrew no longer used in everyday conversation by Jews in the time of Jesus. Jesus spoke Aramaic, the common Semitic language of ancient Palestine at the turn of the millennium. The international language of the day was Greek, and educated people throughout the eastern Mediterranean were trained in Greek. Quite naturally, then, the scriptures of Israel were translated into Aramaic and Greek. The tradition of Aramaic translations is preserved in what are called the *Targumim,* Aramaic for translations. They have little visible influence on the Christian tradition. In contrast, the tradition of Greek translations had a fundamental influence. The dominant Greek translation is called the Septuagint (abbreviated LXX, the Latin numeral for seventy). According to legend, before the time of Christ, Ptolemy, the king of Egypt, commissioned seventy scholars to translate the Old Testament. Each was put into a separate cell and required to produce a full translation of the entire text. The result, the legend continues, was the miraculous production of seventy identical translations, thus certifying that the Greek version is as worthy of veneration as the original Hebrew.[2]

This legend reflects a religious fact: in antiquity, the Septuagint was the dominant form of the Old Testament, both in the Jewish communities throughout the Mediterranean and in the nascent Christian community. In fact, whenever the New Testament writings quote the Old Testament, it is the Septuagint form that is used. What is fascinating, however, is that this dominance, while largely unquestioned (Jerome, who produced the dominant Latin translation of the Old Testament is the exception, for he used the Hebrew rather than the Greek as the basis for his translation), did not foreclose a telling concern about just which words were the right ones. The church fathers presumed the authority of the Septuagint, but they did not confuse authority with clarity. Some Greek words posed problems, and recourse to the Hebrew held out hope of shedding light on difficult words.

Origen provides one of the most notable examples. Without doubt one of the most interesting figures in the Christian tradition, Origen combined a strikingly speculative mind (so much so that some of his theological ideas were eventually condemned) with an equally striking attention to textual detail. He compiled a tool for textual analysis called the *Hexapla,* an edition of the scriptures in which six versions of the same text are presented in parallel columns: Hebrew, a transliteration of the Hebrew into Greek letters, three now lost translations of the Hebrew into Greek by second-century Jews, and the Septuagint. The *Hexapla* survives only in fragments, and we cannot be altogether sure what Origen did with it. Nonetheless, we can reasonably assume that he used it as a comparative tool for discerning just which words were the right words and what those words meant. This is the essence of the lexical strategy.

Origen's *Treatise on the Passover* illustrates the fruit of this strategy of interpretation. In this treatise, Origen promises a word-for-word exegesis of the Exodus account of the Passover. Before taking up the narrative, Origen wishes to set aside a widespread misunderstanding. "Most of the brethren," he writes, "indeed perhaps all, think that the Passover takes its name from the passion of the Savior."[3] This is an understandable assumption, for the Greek verb "to suffer" (*paschein*) is nearly identical with the Greek word for the Passover (*pascha*) used in the translation of Exodus. However, through his study of the original Hebrew, Origen knows that the Greek word used in the Septuagint is a transliteration of a Hebrew word for Passover, not a translation, and the Hebrew word means "passage." It has no connection to suffering. Thus, he warns his readers, "Should one of us in conversation with Hebrew people too rashly mention that the Passover takes its name from the suffering of the Savior, he would be ridiculed by them as one totally ignorant of the meaning of the word."[4] For Origen, the moral is clear and worthy of any contemporary historical scholar: such errors "warn us against rashly attempting to interpret things written in Hebrew without first knowing the Hebrew meaning."[5]

The goal of interpretation is not to avoid mockery. It is to gain insight into what is written. For Origen, the proper lexical understanding of passover (*pascha*) does not simply deliver us from error, it opens the way toward a deeper, fuller understanding. Knowing the textual details, in this case that the source of *pascha* is a transliteration and that there is no semantic connection between passion and passover, forces us to think again and more deeply about the details of the text. If the words *pascha* and *paschein* are not related, then how does the Exodus account of the Passover function in relationship to Jesus Christ? If it is not an anticipation of his passion, then what does Paul mean when he says, "Our paschal lamb, Christ, has been sacrificed" (1 Cor 5:7)?

For Origen, these questions are exactly the right ones, and we must look more closely at the text to find the correct answers. Origen worries that someone who makes the false connection between the suffering of Christ and the Passover might imagine that Jesus' death saves as a moment of ritual sacrifice and then limit the framework for interpreting redemption in Christ to that context. As Origen insists, "the Passover is not a type of the passion but a type of Christ himself."[6] The whole of Christ's life and teaching are related to the Exodus account of the Passover, and redemption entails a full participation in Christ, not the extrinsic application of a sacrificial exchange. Here is his account, interwoven with the Passover account in Exodus 12: "each one of us first takes the lamb, then dedicates it, then sacrifices it, and thus, after roasting it, eats it and after eating it leaves nothing until the morning, and then celebrates the feast of the unleavened bread after having come out of Egypt."[7] We discuss the exegetical technique of weaving an event in the history of Israel together with present experience ("each one of us first takes the lamb") in the next chapter. For the moment, the point is simple. Having blocked a false reading of Israel's Passover as verbally connected to Jesus' passion, Origen turns toward what he envisions as a fuller and more fruitful interpretation of the relationship between the Passover and the saving work of Jesus Christ. This fuller reading forces us to connect the narrative moments of dedication, roasting, eating, and celebration to the manner of our participation in Christ's life, teaching, death, and resurrection.

The way in which Origen expounds this connection between the Passover and Christ's redemptive role is extraordinarily complex and involves other forms of intensive reading, as well as the use of typology and allegory. This short sample is sufficient, however, to show how Origen's lexical investigation of the specific source of the Greek word for the Passover opens the way for a rich interpretation of Christ as the Passover:

> If the lamb is Christ and Christ is the logos, what is the flesh of the divine words if not the divine scriptures? That is what is to be eaten neither raw nor cooked with water. Should, therefore, some cling just to the words themselves, they would eat the flesh of the Savior raw, and partaking of the raw flesh would merit death and not life—it is after the manner of beasts and not humans that they are eating his flesh—since the Apostle teaches us that the letter kills, but the Spirit gives life [2 Cor 3:6]. If the Spirit is given us from God and God is a devouring fire [Deut 4:24,

Heb 12:29], the Spirit is also fire, which is what the Apostle is aware of in exhorting us to be aglow with the Spirit [Rom 12:11]. Therefore, the Holy Spirit is rightly called fire, which it is necessary for us to receive in order to have converse with the flesh of Christ, I mean the divine scriptures, so that, when we have roasted them with this divine fire, we may eat them roasted with fire.[8]

In other words, for Origen, we do not participate in salvation extrinsically as the recipient of a sacrificial offering made on our behalf. The lexical investigation that shows that the Greek *pascha* is a transliteration and not a form of *paschein* blocks this reading of the relationship between the Exodus account and Christ. Rather, the details of the Exodus story are brought into an association with the basic practices of Christian piety, in this case a devotion to reading scripture according to the rule of faith.

Lexical interpretation can be broader than checking up on translations. It also involves creating a mental dictionary of particular uses of key terms. To recall the example we gave, students can better grasp the subtle nuances of Heidegger's concept of being-there if they can recall its use in different contexts. Origen was a master of this lexical strategy as well as the more narrowly technical issues of translation. His exegesis often provides long digressions into how scripture uses various terms. For instance, in the long citation above, Origen provides a thumbnail glossary of scriptural uses of *fire*. He thus builds up a fulsome context or set of contexts for the use of key words. Let us turn to another example and see how this method works.

Origen's *Commentary on the Gospel According to John* was never completed, perhaps because his approach is so exhaustive (and potentially exhausting). His treatment of the first verse of John's gospel, "In the beginning was the Word," involves a word-by-word analysis. Beginning with *beginning* (*arche* in the Greek), Origen reports a truism well known to students of Greek thought: *arche* means many things. To look up *arche* in a dictionary of classical philosophy is to find an array of interrelated meanings ranging from the sense of beginning as origin in time, to beginning as source of substance, to beginning as basis in principle, and so on. For this reason, a translator may use many different English words for *arche:* beginning, source, origin, principle, basis, rule. For Origen, the use of *arche* in the scriptures is just as diverse. As he reports, "if anyone should observe this title, collecting its occurrence from every source, and should wish, by careful examination, to understand its application in each passage of the scriptures, he will discover many meanings of the expression even in the word of God."[9] The intensive reader builds up a mental lexicon.

Origen offers a survey of five different senses of beginning. (1) "One meaning involves change, and this belongs, as it were, to a way and length which is revealed by the scripture: 'the beginning of a good way is to do justice' [Prov 16:7]."[10] Origen has in mind the many ways in which the Bible commends a specific path toward God, defining a point of departure for faithfulness. (2) The second sense of *arche* concerns priority. "There is also a 'beginning' of creation . . . , which would seem to be its use in the statement, 'In the beginning God made heaven and earth' [Gen 1:1]."[11] (3) A further sense turns on the concept of source. "That from which something comes, as the underlying matter, is thought to be a beginning."[12] For Origen, however, there can be no preexistent or underlying matter; God creates everything, and God is not material, so this sense does not apply. (4) *Arche* means more than point of departure, priority in time or being, or material source. "That according to which something is made, as according to its form, is also a beginning," he observes, "since the firstborn of all creation is the image of the invisible God [cf. Col 1:15], the Father is his beginning. And likewise also Christ is the beginning of those made according to the image of God [cf. Gen 1:27]."[13] Here, the sense of *arche* is that of a shaping principle rather than an initial cause, origin as "from this idea or conception" instead of origin as "from this point in time." This is a distinction Origen exploits in his commentary. (5) Finally, "there is also a beginning that pertains to learning, according to which we say that the letters of the alphabet are the beginning of writing. In accordance with this the apostle says, 'Although, because of the time, you should be teachers, you have need that someone teach you again the rudiments of the beginning of the oracles of God' [Heb 5:12]."[14] *Arche* can mean a point of departure.

This array of uses can make our heads spin, but we need not worry overmuch about the specifics of Origen's analysis. Our goal is to see how he uses this lexical exercise. As he turns to the first verse of the Gospel of John, he rules out senses (1), (2), and (5)—he has already set aside (3) in his initial comments. This leaves the fourth sense, *arche* as that principle "by which" something is done, and Origen adopts this meaning to begin an analysis of "In the beginning was the Word." Having settled on the proper sense of *arche*, Origen would seem to be using the lexical strategy in the same way as many modern historical-critical readers: to limit a potentially inconclusive range of options and establish a determinative sense. What seems, however, is not necessarily so, and we need to look more closely at just how Origen uses the lexical strategy.

Origen makes no philological or historical arguments for employing the fourth, formal sense of *arche*. Instead, he offers a justification based upon his overall assessment of scripture's teaching about the incarnate Word. The fourth sense of *arche* coheres with the presumption, widespread among Christian readers, that the Word is wisdom. It is by and through wisdom that God does all things. This presumption, in turn, draws in a key scriptural statement in which *arche* appears, allowing Origen to spin a web of observations that starts to show how to connect the pieces of scripture. Origen reports, "For wisdom says in Solomon, 'God created me the beginning of his ways for his works' [Prov 8:22]."[15] The point, then, of starting with the fourth sense of *arche* is not to fix or limit. Instead, for Origen, if the reader adopts the correct approach to the relationship of the Word as with God in the "beginning" (an approach that, as we shall see in the upcoming discussion of Athanasius, the tradition came to regard as insufficiently precise), then just as filling in a crucial word at the center of a crossword puzzle can initiate a chain of solutions to other difficult words, the reader can make progress toward a "total reading" of scripture.

Origen is keenly aware of this exegetical consequence, so much so that as soon as he establishes the fourth, formal sense of *arche* as the proper "beginning" for interpreting the "beginning" of the Gospel of John (which, in his introduction to the commentary, he has shown to be the "firstfruit" or "beginning" of the gospel, which is itself the "beginning" of our fellowship with God), the other senses immediately flood back into view. After all, if the Word is the wisdom that is the *arche* of the Father's deeds and commandments, then knowing this truth is the "beginning," in the first ("way and length") and fifth ("beginning of the oracle of God") senses. This allows Origen to coherently affirm that Christ is the *arche* of the Father and at the same time "the way, the truth and the life" (John 14:6) for us. Still further, if we allow that the Word is the *arche* of the Father in this fourth sense, then we can explain how the Word who was with God in the beginning [John 1:2] is also the "firstborn of all creation" [Col 1:15]. Even the third sense of *arche,* in which something is the beginning as the material basis, can be recovered. Thus, for Origen, if the Word is the wisdom by which the Father acts and commands, then one might sensibly affirm the plain sense of John 1:3–4, "What came into being in him was life." The incarnate Word is the material basis for salvation; new life comes from him.

For Origen, close attention to the diverse uses of words in scripture does not seek to fix a meaning for a discrete passage by establishing one and only one definition. Origen's goal is to make us aware of the many possible uses of *arche* and in this way to frame the puzzle of the first verse of John in terms of the scripture's larger context. Thus framed, the "solution" sought is global, not local. Origen wants to read John 1:1 in a linguistically responsible fashion. He seeks a reading that adopts a plausible sense for crucial words such as *beginning*. But what is linguistically responsible is not necessarily theologically fruitful, and the latter is determined by the ability of a reading of John 1:1 to support a reading of the scriptures as a whole. To return to Irenaeus' image, Origen uses the lexical strategy to itemize and categorize different pieces of the mosaic in order to prepare the way for a comprehensive reading of the scriptures, taken as a whole.

Origen was among the most disciplined readers in the ancient world. He was patient in describing the differences between the varied elements of scripture, and he foreswore a haphazard and hasty reading, even as he assembled some of the most complex and ambitious interpretations in the early Christian tradition. This unique discipline and virtuosity should not obscure the fact that Origen's approach was widely used throughout the patristic tradition. The church fathers sought a synthetic reading of the whole Bible based upon the hypothesis that Christ fulfills the scriptures, but that synthetic reading was not a jejune exercise conducted at a distance from the semantic details of the biblical text. Patristic readers sought a synthetic reading in and through the details, and this endorsed a vigorous use of lexical commentary. One needs to see the pieces clearly in order to put the puzzle together.

The Dialectical Strategy

Origen's distinctions between the different senses of *arche* already participate in the dialectical strategy. By pulling apart the possible reading of *arche* in John 1:1, he creates a degree of interpretive tension. Which shall it be? How is the preferred sense related to the others? However, in its purest form, the dialectical strategy begins with tensions and contradictions. Origen may satisfy in his ability to draw the different senses of *arche* back into his reading of John 1:1, but he does not need to. A dialectical reading leaves no such option. It seeks out puzzles that do not just tease the mind but also torture the reader with the possibility that a beloved text is corrupted by impossibilities and contradictions.

In the early church, one of the great battles of interpretation concerned the relationship of the incarnate Word, Jesus Christ, to the unchanging and eternal God. One side, associated with Arius, an Alexandrian cleric who lived in the third century, argued that the Son of God was created by God in order to bring salvation. The other side was associated with Athanasius, who as a young man provided some of the crucial arguments that led to the formulation of the Nicene Creed in 325. He argued that the Son of God is an "uncreated person" of the eternal Godhead. This battle was extremely complex, and it involved a wide array of metaphysical and theological issues, none of which we wish to address here.[16] However, like so much of ancient Christian thought, the arguments both pro and con were consistently formulated as exegetical arguments. What interests us about these arguments is not the contributions they made to the emergent Christian doctrine of the Trinity—though this is certainly very important. Rather, we wish to draw attention to the generative function of dialectical reading. The creative aspects of Christian thought on the divine essence were not specified or developed in a speculative mode and then applied to biblical interpretation. Instead, the subtle forms of Trinitarian theology were forged in the process of dialectical interpretation.

A key issue at stake in the debate about the status of the divine Word was a divergent set of biblical passages. One side would seem to suggest that the Word of God is eternal and unoriginate. For example, the first verse of the Gospel of John specifies that "in the beginning was the Word," and the odd verb tense (how can there be a past tense operative "in the beginning"?) encouraged readers such as Athanasius to gloss the verse as follows: "There never was a time when the Word was not." Other biblical passages suggest that the Word of God was created for the specific purpose of effecting salvation. For example, Hebrews 3:2 says that Jesus, whom all in the Arian debate agreed was the incarnate Word of God, "was faithful to the one who appointed [made] him," and Proverbs 8:22, speaking in the voice of divine Wisdom, which as we saw in Origen's exegesis was widely taken to be the divine Word, tells us, "The lord created me at the beginning of his work, the first of his acts long ago." The conflict is patent. Some biblical verses seem to teach that God's Word is eternal, while other verses seem to teach that God's Word is appointed or created at some point in time. The consequence is something like the apparent contradiction in Pascal's famous observation that there are reasons unknown by reason. The two contrasting aspects of scripture suggests that the uncreated Word was created.

Modern readers of the Bible have certainly noticed this apparent contradiction. The solution offered has been to distinguish between two different lines of thought in early Christianity. For example, a modern interpreter might identify the "high Christology" of the author of the Gospel of John and the "adoptionist

Christology" implicit in the Letter to the Hebrews—and reject as illegitimate the notion of reading Proverbs as a text that teaches Christian ideas about the Trinity, since it was written before the time of Jesus. In other words, the modern solution is to say that the contradictory passages come from different books of the Bible written at different times, for different audiences, and for different purposes. As we have emphasized, this solution was not available to early Christian interpreters. They presumed that the Bible was a single witness that, while extremely complex and multifaceted, must be read as a unified whole. Thus, some account had to be given of how it is both true that the Word always "was" (John 1:1) and that the Word was "appointed" (Heb 3:2) and "created" (Prov 8:22).

Historians of early Christianity recognize that the church fathers sought a unified reading. Some champion that endeavor; others regret it as a suppression of the historical diversity and integrity of the various books of the Bible. In this discussion, we are not interested in taking sides. We do, however, want to point out what tends to go unnoticed: the quest for a unified reading of apparently contradictory texts requires conceptual inventiveness and doctrinal innovation. In other words, the dialectical strategy of reading, whether forced upon the church fathers by controversy or sought out for the sheer pleasure of solving puzzles and problems, plays an important creative role in the intellectual development of Christian theology.[17]

In his *Orations against the Arians,* Athanasius takes up the challenge of developing a unified reading of the apparently contradictory descriptions of (to use his terms) the originate or unoriginate character of the Word. These discourses are a complex array of refutations, theological applications, and exegetical digressions. However, the second oration is largely structured by the challenge of harmonizing the verses that suggest the creation (originate status) of the Word with the passages that suggest the eternity (unoriginate status) of the Word. This apparent contradiction between the Word as eternal and the Word as created provides Athanasius occasion to formulate a theological solution. The dialectical juxtaposition encourages intellectually ambitious interpretation.

Athanasius' discussion of Hebrews 3:2 is compact and provides the pattern for his much longer discussion of Proverbs 8:22. The key sticking point in the verse from Hebrews is the immediate impression we have that the passage teaches that Jesus, at some point in time, was "given" or "made" the power of salvation. How can the incarnate Word be "made" when the prologue to the

Gospel of John seems so insistent that he "was" from the beginning? For Athanasius, this is not a simple contradiction of isolated verses. He adduces any number of supporting verses that compound the problem. For example, if the Word was "made," then he is a "work." Yet, we read in Ecclesiastes 12:14 that "God shall bring every work to judgment, including every secret thing, whether good or evil." It would seem absurd to imagine that God needs to judge his own Word. So, the problem is compounded. How can we affirm the literal sense of Hebrews 3:2 that the Word is somehow "made" without creating problems elsewhere in our reading of the Bible, not just in the Johannine literature but in many other places?

Origen's application of the differing senses of *arche* implicitly provides a solution. Establishing the primary sense of *arche* as the form of all things allows him to find a place for the subordinate senses of *arche,* which includes the sense of origin as the initial or beginning moment in time. However, the theological implications remain undeveloped because the question of whether the Word is originate or unoriginate is not sharply drawn in Origen's commentary. Athanasius' approach must meet the controversies of his day. This requires him to explain how to parse the various verses of scripture that appear to conflict. He therefore broadens Origen's lexical approach according to Irenaeus' proposal for reading scripture as part of the divine economy. For Irenaeus, the Bible as a whole teaches the truth about God, but that truth has "essential" and "economic" aspects; the scriptures teach some truths about God that are simply true of God as such. For example, in many places, the scriptures proclaim that God is one. This is always the case. However, the scriptures also teach what God does at particular times. In fact, this is the predominant focus of the scriptures' sequential or narrative shape because the different episodes tell of different moments or dispensations in the divine economy. This distinction between essential and economic truths allows Athanasius to pursue the dialectical strategy to a successful conclusion.

Athanasius develops his reading of the contrast between John 1:1 and Hebrews 3:2 by drawing attention to the fact that the focus of Hebrews, priestly intercession, is a feature of the divine economy that unfolds in space and time with discrete beginnings. He observes that when God provides the means ("the ephod, the breastplate, the robe") by which Aaron may be made a priest, something is done in the temporal sphere that implements God's plan, or the divine economy. Aaron always is a human being (an essential truth), but he is made a priest (an economic truth). This textual observation allows Athanasius to return to the apparent contradiction between John 1:1 and Hebrews 3:2. The former teaches something essential. The Word always is the eternally begotten Son of the Father. The latter teaches something economic. As Athanasius observes, "When the Father willed that ransoms should be paid for all and to all, grace should be given, then truly the Word, as Aaron his robe, so did he take on flesh."[18] Just as one can say that Aaron always was a human being but became a high priest for his people, so also can one say that the Word of God always was the Word of God (e.g., John 1:1) but became a high priest for all humanity (e.g., Heb 3:2).

We tend to read figures such as Athanasius with the retrospective knowledge of the development and communal endorsement of his approach. This encourages us to think of the exegesis in treatises such as the *Orations against the Arians* as attempts to resolve unfortunate textual difficulties that stand in the way of "orthodox doctrine." Worse, we might even think that Irenaeus is applying an extrinsic body of propositions called "orthodox doctrine" to the biblical text as a "solution." Both tendencies fail to see how a technical distinction in Christian theology, in this case the distinction between essence and economy, function within the exegesis rather than operating upon it from the outside, either as something to be defended or applied. For Athanasius, what commends use of Irenaeus' notion of economy is its exegetical fruitfulness. One can resolve the apparent contradiction in the text by recourse to the distinction between essence and economy. Thus, it would be more accurate to say that the kind of problem posed by John 1:1 over and against Hebrews 3:2 produced "orthodox doctrine" rather than to think of this problem as something cleared up by certain theological convictions that existed prior to and independently of exegetical puzzles.[19]

Athanasius' prior commitments to certain ideas about God and the Word of God shape his analysis. We are not arguing that his consideration of the conflict between John 1:1 and Hebrews 3:2 was temporally prior to his conviction that one can distinguish between who God is (essence) and what God does (economy). Our claim is more subtle. In his *Orations*, Athanasius positively dwells on problems posed by contrasting verses rather than rushing to resolve them, and he does so because the interpretive mentality of church fathers was largely different from our own. We tend to treat theological doctrines as established propositions. We then approach the scriptures as a source of data by which to "prove" or "disprove" the doctrines. Athanasius was one of the crucial supporters of the Nicene Creed, and his influence may have been one of the single most important causes of its subsequent adoption by the church as a touchstone of orthodoxy.

Nonetheless, in his refutation of the Arians, Athanasius does not so much "prove" the Nicene doctrine as demonstrate its exegetical effectiveness. The Arians can harmonize John 1:1 with Hebrews 3:2 with their own emendations and distinctions, but the consequence, Athanasius argues, is an impoverished position for thinking through any number of secondary and tertiary verses (e.g., Eccles 12:14, which teaches that God will judge all his works). He claims that his approach resolves the apparent contradiction in a fashion that illuminates the inner coherence of the scriptures, a coherence that has a far greater verbal and spiritual density than merely distinguishing between essence and economy. Thus, for Athanasius, what is prior is the urgency of a unified, coherent reading of scripture, a reading that maximizes the number of unstrained interpretations of individual words, verses, and episodes. Doctrine "follows" from that priority. However much we might already presume certain doctrines, it is the ability of those theological judgments to advance our unified reading and deepen our sense of the coherence of scripture that gives credence.

Athanasius' treatment of Proverbs 8:22 demonstrates. The verse has wisdom (recall that Athanasius equates wisdom with the Word) created by God as the beginning of his works. Against the background of Plato's *Timaeus,* the plain sense of the verse, as well as the immediate context, seems to portray wisdom as a divine demiurge made by the eternal God as an instrument for the fashioning of all finite things. After citing Proverbs 8:22, Athanasius assembles a wide array of passages that suggest the eternity of the divine Word, and this, of course, points toward the difficulty of reading Proverbs in a Platonic fashion. Yet, he is not measuring out scriptural citations, as if pros might outweigh the cons. The decisive question is the structure of interpretation that allows one to read all the passages as teaching something true about God and His ways.

The basic conceptual strategy follows the treatment of Hebrews 3:2. Since Athanasius distinguishes between divine essence and divine economy, he can affirm the eternity of the Word of God and, at the same time, affirm that the Word is the means by which God does things in the created order. Through the Word, God "makes" the divine economy. What is important, however, is that the solution is not conceptual. The concepts of essence and economy serve the exegesis, and the cumulative effect of Athanasius' successful use of these concepts in the management of the diversity of scripture constitutes the solution to the problem posed by the contradictory verses. Athanasius provides extended exegetical demonstrations of the fruitfulness of distinguishing between the eternal Word whose essence is to be with the Father, and the divine economy in which the Word is the "beginning of his works." Using the immediate context of Proverbs, Athanasius shows how this distinction allows one to see how Proverbs 9:1 ("Wisdom has built her a house") refers to the way in which the incarnate Word has come into the world in order to save us in our bodies. This leads to an extensive list of biblical verses, each of which specify in different idioms the saving work of Christ: to defeat the devil (e.g., Heb 2:15), overcome death (e.g., 1 Cor 15:21), fulfill the law (e.g., Rom 8:4), save the world (e.g., John 3:17), restore sight (e.g., John 9:39), break down the wall of hostility (Eph 2:14). The divine economy is as richly diverse as the divine essence is singular.

Exploring how contradiction motivates distinctions that, in turn, illuminate other portions of the scripture is the goal of the dialectical strategy. Athanasius does not discount one side of the contradiction in order to sustain the other side. The solution he offers allows him to focus on interpreting the passages that would seem most troublesome for his own affirmation of the unchanging, uncreated, and eternal status of the Word. The result is not a stance that allows Athanasius to say "I told you so" to his adversaries. Instead, distinction between essence and economy provides the basis for a Logos or Christ-centered account of the countless biblical passages that concern the "making" and "creating" that God does in the temporal world. Athanasius need not stage-manage these specific passages into a single account of just who the Word of God is (e.g., how can the eternal Son of God *be* the high priest who fulfills the law *before* the law is given on Sinai?). Nor does Athanasius try to bring the verses into a single account of how the Word saves (e.g., is it the sacrifice of his death or the triumph of the resurrection?). The distinction between essence and economy allows him to order his interpretation so that the self-evidently different verses can say something legitimately different, yet function as part of a coherent, comprehensive reading.

In this way, despite the extremely heated controversy with the Arians, Athanasius' exegesis of seemingly contradictory passages is marked by an interest in the coherence of scripture for its own sake and not simply for the sake of gaining a polemical upper hand. The pressure of apparent contradiction forces a closer examination of the scriptural texts, and, perhaps more importantly, it also forces a reexamination of the larger framework of assumptions that govern our reading of the Bible. Of course, we may conclude that Athanasius was mistaken. By and large, modern scholars would utterly reject his solution, preferring explanations of divergent scriptural texts that depend upon observations about historical and cultural changes. Yet, whatever the outcome, our views are not unchanged. Just as modern theories of historical development provide an integrative framework that gives an intellectually satisfying account of the diversity of scripture, Athanasius' distinction between divine essence and divine economy provides an interpretive strategy that integrates the breadth of scripture into a single account. The difference is that Athanasius' integrative framework, which is representative of the patristic tradition and so unlike the modern historical approach, requires us to discipline our ideas about God and the identity of Jesus Christ as the incarnate Word. To follow Athanasius' interpretive lead, we must think clearly about God.

Associative Strategies

Although specific interpretations no doubt differ because the interpretive resources and assumptions differ, the lexical and dialectical strategies that characterize patristic exegesis are widely used by modern readers. We can hardly imagine reading the Bible without lexical aids, and countless scholarly monographs take the basic form of showing the difficulty of a unified interpretation of the Bible and offering an explanation. This is less true for the associative strategy. By and large, modern readers distrust the ways in which words are easily connected simply on the basis of verbal echoes and patterns. For example, in one of his digressive comments on Proverbs 8:22, Athanasius exploits a phrase in the verse ("beginning of his ways") to establish a link to Colossians 1:15 ("first-born of all creation"), and this, in turn, provides the basis for an extended meditation on the Christ-like shape of the divine economy. Modern scholars shrink from the purely verbal nature of the link, and they are careful to restrict themselves to discussing discrete historical periods and literary contexts. Ancient readers had the opposite reaction. They positively relished the way verbal associations can motivate leaps from one context to another. The same sensibility that makes us chuckle when we hear a clever pun was given much freer rein in patristic exegesis.

Cyril of Alexandria opens his *Commentary on the Gospel of John* with a characteristic observation that discerning the mysteries of God is a difficult task fraught with peril. Yet we need not despair. Drawing on Psalm 68:11 (LXX), Cyril reports that God promises to give words to those who seek to speak His commandments.[20] However, Cyril does not treat the matter as resolved, as if a single "proof text" might secure his position. He shifts into a different scriptural idiom and quotes a passage from Ecclesiastes 10:9–10 that offers practical advice: "Whoever splits wood will be endangered thereby; if the iron is blunt, and he does not sharpen the edge and he shall be troubled and work harder."[21] This would seem irrelevant to the practical task of reading, but Cyril observes that the word *wood* means the content of holy scripture. With this substitution, Cyril is able to link the ax to the reader. Scripture is, indeed, difficult to understand, and we can be troubled and burdened by the work of interpretation. But if we keep our minds sharpened with the "right perception" that is born of following the "straight path," then God will give us the words we need to teach others what the scriptures truly mean.

This is an instance of the associative strategy. Cyril is concerned about the dangers of a careless, lazy approach to interpretation, and with the association of *wood* with scripture, he is able to utilize the passage from Ecclesiastes to address this concern. Yet Cyril does not drop the thread of association; he follows the theme of wood and axes into a different part of scripture, citing Deuteronomy 20:19–20 where Moses instructs the Israelites on the laws of warfare, telling them that they are not to put axes to the trees of a captured city, for they have value as a source of fruit. One is only to cut down the trees that bear no fruit. Cyril reinforces this teaching with other verses from Deuteronomy that command the people of Israel to destroy the groves around the idolatrous altars. He is so eager to exploit that verbal association that he takes Paul's agricultural analogies of plowing and threshing in 1 Corinthians 9:9–10 and imports the word *trees* into his paraphrase of the verse. His network of scriptural passages both commend the preservation and cultivation of "wood" and urge its destruction. We have already seen how the dialectical strategy exploits apparent conflicts (should we preserve or cut down the trees?), and it appears that Cyril is assembling passages according to a verbal and thematic association in order to set up an apparent conflict that will require resolution.

What is the solution? For Cyril, the preserving and destroying of forests teaches us how to approach scripture. We should follow Moses' teaching and approach with a discerning spirit the writings of those who teach falsely. Cyril warns against "cutting down" the very words of scripture that are ill used by the heretics. Although he never formulates it so generally, his message would seem to be: Avoid a campaign of destroying falsehood that is so comprehensive that truths of scripture are also lost. This is not a counsel of complacency. Staying with the image of fruit-bearing plants, Cyril cites Hosea 8:7: "A stalk having no strength to yield meal, if so be its yield, the strangers shall swallow it up." The weak and foolish are often deceived into consuming fruitless teaching, and for this reason the orthodox teacher rightly seeks to put the ax to false teaching even as he preserves the scriptural verses that are being ill used. The interpreter who follows this advice will proceed as did Athanasius, refuting false interpretation, but preserving and integrating the scriptural verses favored by the heretics into a more comprehensive interpretation.

The associative chain does not end here. Cyril's interpretive imagination continues to play upon the purely verbal possibilities of the scriptures. He leaves behind his dependence upon "wood" and "trees," and he fixes his attention on the fruit that justifies preserving the groves of those conquered in times of war. Cyril returns to the opening theme. He reminds his readers of his unworthiness as an interpreter, suggesting that silence might be the better way. However, he must respond to the needs of others. Echoing Hebrews 13:15, he promises to offer the "fruit" of his "lips" as a "spiritual sacrifice." He ends his introduction to the commentary by taking consolation in God's modest and reasonable expectations, citing Leviticus 1:14 ("he shall bring his offering of turtledoves or of young pigeons") and Leviticus 2:1 ("his offering shall be fine flour"). Thus, he has warned his readers of the great difficulty of right reading of scripture; he has instructed them on the need to distinguish true from false teaching with a discerning "ax"; he has exhorted them not to cut down the fruit-bearing verses of scripture that have fallen into the hands of heretics; and he has consoled them that the Lord accepts the fruit of their (and his) modest exegetical insights.

Though we may or may not agree with the sentiments expressed, we must stay focused on the associative strategy. We need to see and understand how Cyril constructs his remarks. He uses the purely verbal connection of wood to the content of scripture. He expands the association to encompass passages that concern those trees that are fruit bearing and non–fruit bearing, extending the image to include stalks of wheat. Then, drawing upon the sacrificial imagery of the Letter to the Hebrews, he shifts from discussing the trees as sources of bounty and nourishment to their use as sacrifices to God. Now he can turn to Leviticus for verses that concern the reassuringly modest resources one needs for an acceptable sacrifice.

This small portion from the introduction to Cyril's Commentary on the *Gospel According to John* is very typical of the patristic tradition, and, in our experience, the strategy of association that it so effectively illustrates is for modern readers the most objectionable and alienating aspect of patristic exegesis. We might balk at any of these steps. We might reject the notion that words in scripture might mean something other than their literal sense, e.g., that *wood* means "teaching of scripture." We might rebel against his slide from fruit trees to a more general notion of life-giving food. We might find the final jump to Leviticus a strain. We might find ourselves exasperated by what we imagine to be the sheer arbitrariness of every interpretive move. All these hesitations typify modern responses to patristic exegesis. At this point, we can only suggest why Cyril and the rest of the fathers were motivated to construct extensive networks of association. The associative strategy is a method of intensive reading that serves two goals. It enhances the breadth of patristic exegesis, thus advancing the agenda of a comprehensive or total reading of scripture, and it contributes to the depth of interpretation that the church fathers sought at every turn.

Like the lexical and dialectical strategies, the associative approach operates at a profoundly local level by focusing on particular words and images. These local strategies, however, serve the larger goal of patristic exegesis. We saw how Origen not only itemizes the possible meanings of *arche* but also integrates them into a comprehensive reading. The same occurs in Athanasius' approach to the verses that argue both for and against the unoriginate status of the Word. His distinction between essence and economy not only resolves the troubling verses but structures his approach to diverse portions of scripture. How strategies of intensive reading provide pieces for the grand mosaic of a total reading of scripture is even more evident in the use of the associative strategy. Cyril's associations range across the canon, from the wisdom literature to the Pentateuch to the Pauline letters. The mere occurrence of a word such as *wood* is a sufficient basis for an associative connection. The effect is to draw scripture into a moment of verbal contemporaneity. From Genesis to Revelation, verbal echoes can be heard across all the differences of time, genre, and even subject matter. For the fathers, the associative strategy functioned like so many thin threads of connection between the disparate portions of scripture. Taken individually, no one association could hold the scriptures together as a single whole. As we have seen with Cyril, however, the fathers pursued associations by the bundle. Taken together, the unifying effect can be strong. In this way, the associative strategy served the broad patristic goal of providing Christ-centered, comprehensive interpretation of scripture.

In early Christian exegesis, the associative strategy functioned in countless ways, not only because the human mind is endlessly inventive but also because the church fathers thought scripture always worthy of more intensive scrutiny. As John Chrysostom reminds his listeners in a homily, one cannot "overread" the Bible. "For, just as with grains of incense, the more they are moved about with your fingers, the greater the fragrance they give out," he writes, "so it is with the scriptures in our experience; the more you devote to studying them, the more you are able to discover the treasure hidden in them, and thereby gain great and unspeakable wealth."[22] Chrysostom's assessment was widely shared among early Christian readers. They thought the scriptures infinitely rich, and, for them, interpretive adventure beckoned in every word and image. They sought to rub verses together with the associative strategy in order to evoke the sweet fragrance of insight.

Words are remarkable artifacts. A word such as *gray* might denote a color, suggest a mood, or serve as last name. To a certain extent, the modern age has rebelled against the diverse potency of words and their fragrance. One influential nineteenth-century scholar, Benjamin Jowett, expressed a characteristic anxiety when he criticized the church fathers for their strategies of intensive reading, especially the associative strategy. For Jowett, "If words have more than one meaning, they may have any meaning."[23] The notion that we might read Deuteronomy and its teaching on the obligations of the Israelites to cut down or preserve trees and then leap to refutations of false teaching and preservation of scriptural truths would strike Jowett, and many contemporary readers, as whimsical at best and willful at worst. For this reason, while modern readers use the lexical strategy, more often than not, the goal is to settle on one and only one definition of key terms. Origen's creative combination of the relevant definitions of *arche* in his exegesis of the opening of the Gospel of John would seem to betray the real potential of the lexical strategy: to limit the possibilities of meaning.

One of the most important changes in contemporary intellectual culture has been the eclipse of Jowett's characteristically modern prejudices about language. Instead of regretting the remarkable ability of words to generate multiple meanings, postmodern literary theory champions the ways in which specific words and images function more like intersections of forces than placeholders for determinate and fixed meanings. Today, we assume that words are historically saturated. They have a shaping force that can influence attitudes and behaviors. In fact, contemporary society seems so convinced of the associative potency of words that the use of masculine pronouns is much curtailed. We associate the use of *mankind* with oppressive social mores, and we worry words can echo in our consciousness and distort self-images, as well as in society, leading to oppressive behaviors. To avoid these consequences, we exercise as much verbal care as the church fathers. The difference, however, is that we are more likely to step back from the potency of words—or to use that potency to dance deconstructive rings around modern figures such as Jowett. Postmodern readers may wish to rub words together, as Chrysostom suggested, but those same postmodern readers do not think that there are sacred texts with spirit-saturated words that contain an unspeakably great fragrance. The fathers did, and they believed that the fragrance was not only pleasant, it had the sweet odor of sacrifice that rose up to the heavens.

CHAPTER FOUR

Typological Interpretation

> The connection between occurrences is not regarded as primarily a chrono-
> logical or causal development but as a oneness within the divine plan.
>
> ERICH AUERBACH, *Mimesis*

We turn now to a consideration of typology. The fathers did not adopt a consistent technical vocabulary to describe their interpretive efforts. However, we
adopt the term *typology* to draw attention to the practice by which the fathers
moved beyond analysis of particular words and images toward the larger, unifying patterns of the Bible. They understood scripture to be a part of the divine
economy. As we saw with Irenaeus, this belief led to the presumption that the
Bible possessed an ordered sequence. The body of biblical particularity had a
distinct architecture to be discerned and expounded. Furthermore, they took
their faith in Christ as the recapitulation of the divine plan. Christ was the
interpretive key; the larger coherence of scripture was structured by the figure of
Christ. They used typological exegesis to explore this larger coherence and
describe the architecture of the text. It allowed them to develop a unified reading of the Old and New Testaments, as well as provided a means to bring Christian practice and experience into the structured economy of the scriptures, all
drawing upon the central figure of Christ. For this reason, typological interpretation is rightly viewed as the most important interpretive strategy for early
Christianity. Without typology it is difficult to imagine patristic theology and
the concept of Christian orthodoxy it defined and supported as existing at all.

The term *typology* comes from the Greek *typos,* a word that ranges in meaning from the specific sense found in *typewriter* or *typeface,* to the broad sense of form, figure, or pattern. We often say that an actor whose personality fits the role is "typecast." The prototype made in the inventor's shop is the original that will serve as the basis for mass production. After a friend comes late yet again, we might throw our hands up and say, "typical," or "it figures." Events can be analyzed according to type. For example, when a pitcher throws a no-hitter, the term denotes a type. So, marks on a page can follow a set "type"; physical objects that have a common pattern are of the same "type"; people can have personalities that follow a "type"; events can be categorized by "type." This remarkable range demonstrates the power of typological exegesis.

Typological interpretation of the Bible is present in every century of Christian history, and the reason is straightforward. Types transcend distances of time and space and help to create a sense of participation in a unified reality or, to use Irenaeus' term, economy. A no-hitter pitched in Chicago in the 1920s can be linked to a no-hitter pitched last year in Boston. A common type draws them together. The same holds with Biblical types. On the last day of his life, Martin Luther King delivered what proved to be a prophetic speech. "I have been to the mountain top," he declared, "and I have seen the Promised Land." When he said this, he was using typology. He was associating the civil rights movement with the divinely guided deliverance of the Israelites out of their slavery in Egypt.

The historical distances separating King from Moses are so vast that the possibility of connecting the two seems impossible. Moses, if he existed at all, lived in the ancient Near East. As a hero of ancient Israel, he led the Israelites out of their captivity and into a generation of wandering in the deserts of Sinai. At the end of his life Moses ascended Mount Nebo, gazed upon the land of Canaan, and ceded leadership to Joshua who would lead the people across the Jordan to conquer the Promised Land. King, on the other hand, fought no wars of liberation and struggled for the inheritance of no land. He ascended no actual mountain. Although he was a hero of the twentieth-century American civil rights movement, he practiced a strictly nonviolent form of resistance at odds with the liberating tactics of the Israelites as they entered the Promised Land.

In spite of all the differences, a common shape or pattern obtains, or so King wished to suggest. The success of King's oration does not depend upon direct correspondences between the referenced history of ancient Israel and the details of the civil right struggle. Instead, he is appealing to a common type. He may not have ascended any actual mountain, but in his eyes the civil rights movement was a long difficult uphill struggle. He wished to communicate his confidence that the struggle would end successfully and that the promise of the Declaration of Independence—that all men are created equal—would be fulfilled. Moreover, the speech has a special and unintended typological power because King, like Moses, was unable to enter into the future that he envisioned.

The associations that King calls to mind in his speech are the essence of typological interpretation. By implicitly comparing the liberation of American blacks to the struggle of the ancient Israelites to escape from the bondage of slavery in Egypt, the civil rights struggle is drawn into the divine economy and becomes an extension of it. Those familiar with the story of the Exodus need not be told the narrative details in order to recognize King's appeal to the type. No special reading of Exodus was necessary for King's supporters to understand that the defenders of segregation were like the Egyptians who had hardened their hearts against God's will. Likewise, all familiar with the story would have felt some sense of foreboding at King's reference to Mount Nebo, where Moses died within sight of the Promised Land.

Typological associations of the sort advanced by King remain extraordinarily common, even in our postcritical culture, and should not be dismissed as relics of the past. However, because they are often practiced in distinctly nonreligious ways, we fail to notice them as typologies. Whenever somebody alludes to an event in a shared cultural narrative as a means of illuminating the present, that individual is using typology. For instance, in the 1970s there was a television show called *The Brady Bunch*. TV Land, a cable network dedicated to nostalgia, has ensured that a whole new generation of American children has seen and at least partially internalized the narrative world of Mike, Carol, Greg, Marcia, Peter, Jan, Bobby, Cindy, and, of course, Alice. So, if we were to say to a child of the 1970s or a rerun junkie who is feeling particularly insecure, "you are having a Jan Brady moment," she would know the meaning. Indeed, when tried in class, our students inevitably say something like, "right, Marcia, Marcia, Marcia. I get it."

If you have never seen the show, then the typology must be explained. In order to understand why the phrase "a Jan Brady moment" evokes the response "Marcia, Marcia, Marcia," you would have to know about the episode when Jan broke down in a massive fit of teen-age angst and found herself wanting in comparison to her beautiful, blond, older sister Marcia. To Jan everything was about Marcia and nothing was about her. Hence, Jan's anxious sob: "Marcia, Marcia, Marcia."

This attempt to explain the "Jan Brady moment" brings out the most important feature of typological interpretation. A failed typology is one that needs to be explained, and a typology that becomes so theoretical that it sounds like an explanation is no longer a typology at all but rather what we will call an allegory. The beauty of typology is that it allows us, the reader (or viewer), to enter into the experience of the type directly and without the mediation of extended interpretive explanation. We could describe the experience of a person having a "Jan Brady moment" in psychological terms. Such a person might be said to be experiencing anxiety, or early stages of depression, or chronic insecurity, or something much more mundane like normal adolescent ego development. Yet, when we hear "Marcia, Marcia, Marcia," and recognize our own experience as participating in the type without the intervention of mediating ideas, typology is functioning at its best.

The same holds for Martin Luther King's typology. He did not offer a sociological, political, or even theological apparatus to justify the link between the civil rights movement and the Exodus. He articulated the link, and that simply is the interpretation. If successful, the association of the two elements discloses the shared type, and that shared type becomes visible and persuasive to the reader or listener. The dense particularity of the two sides of the typological interpretation does all the work of illumination. The distinctive features of the civil rights movement cast a fresh light on our reading of Exodus; the structure and narrative detail of the Exodus story shapes our take on the civil rights movement.

As we noted above, just how two different phenomena—Exodus and the civil rights movement, or a fictional TV character from the 1970s and the very real personal lives of our students—can function in a mutually illuminating relationship is difficult to explain in theoretical terms that a modern reader would find satisfying. Nonetheless, like the associative strategy with words, the church fathers constantly used this approach. They did so under the guidance of the theological convictions Irenaeus explained. Convinced that the scriptures (and, for that matter, all finite phenomena) were ordered by God according to a coherent plan or economy, the fathers felt confident that the patterns that link seemingly disparate people, artifacts, or events were as real as the "2, 4, 6, 8" that would lead us to continue "10, 12, 14." Moreover, since God has summed up or recapitulated this economy in Jesus Christ, early Christian interpreters thought that they possessed something like the "$x + 2$," the formula that could guide us to identify the real patterns in any set of scriptural data. The upshot of these convictions is a positive zeal for finding typological connections. A reader of the scriptures shows that the divine economy is recapitulated in Christ precisely by showing the countless instances in which specific details of the scripture are linked in a common pattern or type.

The church fathers' typological imagination was wide ranging. We limit ourselves to three patterns of typology, each of which play an important role in early Christian development of a detailed account of the divine economy. The first is the most central. It is an explicit display of the prefiguration of Christ in the Old Testament. The fathers were engaged in a complex double project: first, showing how Christ recapitulates that to which the Old Testament bears witness, and second, to illuminate the identity of Jesus Christ. The second use of typology sought to establish the scriptural basis for the practices of the early church. The upshot was a demonstration that the Christian church functions both in continuity with the chosen children of Abraham and according to the pattern established by Christ. In the third typological endeavor, the fathers used scriptural patterns from both Testaments to integrate the contemporary experience of Christians into those patterns. Instead of discerning "Jan Brady moments," they read their lives and the history of the church as a series of "Jesus moments."

Types of Christ

One of the basic goals of early Christian exegesis was to situate Christ himself within the sacred narratives of the past in the sense that he both participates in and fulfills those narratives. A selection from the homilies of John Chrysostom captures this nicely. In Homily 10, Chrysostom discusses Genesis 1:27–28, a text describing the creation of man in the image of God and the bestowal to the man of dominion over all creation. Chrysostom points out that in Genesis 1:26 the text says that *they* have dominion before the text says anything about the creation of male and female. What could this mean? Chrysostom takes this as an instance of a widespread Biblical pattern. "Such, after all, is the way with all the biblical authors, to speak of things not yet created as though already created," observes Chrysostom. "You see," he clarifies, "since they perceive with the eyes of the spirit things due to happen after a great number of years, and accordingly view things as though already laid out in front of their very eyes, they describe everything in this way."[1] For Chrysostom, the biblical authors, guided by the divine plan, built typological significance into the scriptures. In a sense, all that remains for the interpreter is to recognize the proper patterns of meaning and reference. In his homily Chrysostom turns to Psalm 22 to prove the anticipatory structure of scripture. The ability of the writer of Psalm 22 to anticipate Christ—"they pierce my hands and my feet" and "they divided up my garments among themselves"—is for Chrysostom decisive evidence.

In the New Testament there are several strong typological associations linking Jesus to figures from the Old Testament, all of which the fathers used extensively. An Adam/Jesus link is based upon Paul's pairing of them as pivot points in the divine economy: "For since death came through a human being, the resurrection of the dead has also come through a human being; for as all die in Adam, so all will be made alive in Christ" (1 Cor 15:21–22). Adam, for Paul, "is a type of the one who was to come" (Rom 5:14). The link between David and Jesus is clearly present in the synoptic gospels, and this is also developed more fully in early Christian interpretation. We wish, however, to focus on the connection between Jesus and Joshua because in this instance the church fathers extend typology beyond those immediately suggested by the apostolic witness of the New Testament. Moreover, in the Joshua/Jesus link we can see how a semantic connection is expanded into a typological connection. For in patristic literature Joshua is nearly universally interpreted as a type of Christ, largely because the Septuagint rendered Joshua's name *Iesous,* the same name used for Jesus in the New Testament. This verbal hint is pursued, and a material or narrative pattern emerges that joins Jesus of Nazareth to Jesus son of Nun, who succeeded Moses and led the Israelites across the Jordan and into the Promised Land. In this way, the interpretation becomes typological.

Justin Martyr developed this reading of Joshua in his *Dialogue with Trypho.* In the literary construct of the dialogue, Justin, the Christian, and Trypho, the Jew, are locked for several hundred pages in a sustained exegetical sparring about the true meaning of the scriptures. Justin attempts to prove to Trypho that the scriptures of Israel are about Christ. His typological reflection on the name Joshua is a small part of this effort, which is extensive and defies epitome. Because he and Trypho know the narrative, Justin can make his points directly and gallops through a series of typological associations. He points to the verbal link of the common name, Joshua with Jesus.[2] He observes that Joshua led the

Israelites to victory while Moses sat on a hill with arms outstretched, "which," Justin insists, "was a type of nothing but the cross."[3] The red rope that Rehab, the prostitute of Jericho, used to allow Joshua's spies to escape was also "a symbol of the blood of Christ, by which those of every nationality who were once fornicators and sinful are redeemed."[4] These links reinforce Justin's larger goal of proving that a Christ-centered reading of scripture is the best reading.

In addition to the ad hoc connections in the *Dialogue,* Justin develops an extended reading of Joshua's role as leader of the Israelites. The interpretations are multifaceted, and Justin develops each dimension to bring out the role of Jesus as the fulfilling figure in the divine economy. Joshua anticipates as a figure awaiting fulfillment. First, he highlights that Joshua, and not Moses, led the Israelites into the Promised Land.[5] According to Justin, this shows that Jesus alone can lead all people to salvation: "For, Joshua gave them an inheritance for a time only, since he was not Christ our God, nor the Son of God; but Jesus, after the holy resurrection, will give us an inheritance for eternity."[6] To use Irenaeus' concept of recapitulation, for Justin, Jesus "sums up" the pattern of deliverance found in Joshua by fully enacting it. By this reading, Jesus is to Joshua as Joshua is to Moses. At each stage the divine economy unfolds towards its fulfillment.

Justin further extends the typological scheme according to the same logic. The fifth chapter of the book of Joshua states that the Lord commanded Joshua to circumcise the Israelites "a second time" (Josh 5:2). According to the biblical narrative, Joshua makes "stone knives" and fulfills God's command. Justin begins his textual analysis with an intensive reading of *stone*. "I have already pointed out," he writes, "that the Prophets used to call [Christ] figuratively a Stone and Rock."[7] This lexical specification warrants a reading of the "stone knives" as referring to the teachings of Christ, "by which so many who were in error have been circumcised from their uncircumcision with the circumcision of the heart."[8] More broadly, then, this episode in the book of Joshua 5:2–7, itself a constituent element of the narrative of transition from wilderness to promised land, is read by Justin as a type or prefiguration. It shows how the teachings of Christ supersede the covenant of circumcision. Still further, the passage is a type for Justin himself, who, following the teachings of Christ, turned away from idolatry and other forms of sin.[9] In this way, Justin claims to render the deepest and truest meaning of the passage.

There are two elements of Justin's interpretation of Joshua 5:2–7 that we need to bear in mind. First, his reading is unequivocally and unashamedly retrospective. Justin is operating with something like Irenaeus' view of the divine economy that culminates in Jesus Christ. He treats the apostolic witness to Jesus Christ as the privileged basis for thinking through the logic, import, and structure of many different Old Testament texts. His interlocutor, Trypho the Jew, refuses to accept this privileged point of departure. Justin sees clearly that this refusal will prevent Trypho from accepting the proposed interpretations. "You fail to grasp the meaning of my words," he writes, "because you do not know the things which, it was foretold, Christ would do, nor do you believe us when we refer you to the Scriptures."[10] In other words, for Justin, Trypho reads an episode such as circumcision with stone knives as one might read a series "2, 4, . . ." The real pattern or "type" is unclear. Only when we grasp that Jesus Christ is "6" will we accurately complete the series and grasp the pattern or type.

The inherently retrospective logic of typological reading leads directly into the second point we need to keep in mind. The church fathers did not understand typological exegesis as proof in a narrow or direct sense. Justin does not imagine that his typological exegesis of the stone knives of circumcision in Joshua 5:2 will somehow demonstrate that Jesus fulfills the scriptures. What makes patristic exegesis so difficult to read is that for all early Christian interpreters, the exegetical arguments are cumulative. Justin slides from biblical verse to biblical verse, from outstretched arms of Moses, to the prophetic use of the word *stone* or *rock,* to the shared name *Jesus,* to countless other narrative episodes, scriptural conventions, prophetic passages, and semantic hints, all the while building his case for an integrated reading of the entire Old Testament in and through connections to Jesus Christ. In this way, for Justin, and for the church fathers as a whole, typological interpretation is best understood as an ever-expanding network of patterns and associations that refer back to the apostolic witness about Jesus Christ. The local types—in this instance Joshua/Jesus—function to illuminate how Jesus is the global or master type, the recapitulation of all things.

Justin's *Dialogue with Trypho* is structured as an argument against one who accepts the authority of scripture but not Jesus as the promised Messiah. As a result, the flow of analysis is from Jesus Christ back and into the scriptural text. Most early Christian interpretation was written for readers who already shared a faith in Jesus as the Christ, so it often has a strong forward flow. For example, in Origen's *Homilies on the Book of Joshua*, we find interpretation that shares exactly the same logic as Justin's but more clearly demonstrates how typological exegesis of the Old Testament is not unidirectional. The type does not just explain Joshua, it also clarifies the full role of Jesus as savior.

In the beginning of his first homily on the book of Joshua, Origen, like Justin, observes the semantic identity of "Iesous" of the Old Testament and "Iesous" of the New. On the basis of this verbal identity, he undertakes an extended typological investigation, drawing attention to many of the same aspects of the text that Justin uses in his interpretation. However, in contrast to Justin, Origen emphasizes how typological interpretation illuminates Christ. As he draws back for a moment from the details of the text, Origen observes, "the book of Joshua is designed not so much to know the actions of Joshua son of Nun, but to describe for us the mysteries of Jesus my lord."[11] His point is not to deny that the book of Joshua accurately narrates historical events. Origen, like all early Christian readers of scripture, has little reason to doubt that Joshua existed, succeeded Moses as leader of the Israelites, and led them across the Jordan river. Origen's remark should be understood as a statement about interpretive direction. The text tells of events in the divine economy, in this case Joshua's leadership. The import of these events is not clear until they are typologically linked to another set of events that occurs later in the divine economy. Just as importantly, the later events are themselves not fully clear until the illuminating typological link is established. More succinctly, one learns about Jesus by reading about Joshua. The typology casts light forward as well as backward.

The details of Origen's exegesis bear out this commitment to using typology to better understand the redemptive work of Christ. Like Justin, Origen treats Joshua's supersession of Moses as leader of Israel as a type for the replacement of the old law of Moses by the new law of Christ. He describes Moses' death as a type for the death of the Law: "He is therefore dead, Moses, the servant of God, because the Law is dead and the commandments of the Law therefore have ended."[12] Unlike Justin, however, Origen does not regard this supersession itself as a theological truth that needs no further illumination. Origen seeks to advance his thought through the type. He turns to the passage in Romans where Paul teaches that a woman whose husband has died can remarry because she is released from the law that binds her to her first husband (Rom 7:2–3). Origen treats this detail of the New Testament as a figure for the release of Christian believers from the duties that bind them to the Law. In this way, the typological link of Moses' death to Paul's teaching about remarriage after the death of a spouse serves to place the Old Testament and New Testament within a common typological framework. Both Romans and the book of Joshua testify to the logic of the divine economy in which the coming of Jesus brings the time of the Law to an end and initiates a "new marriage" of God to his people.

This is the turning point in the homily, and as Origen continues he draws attention to many details that distinguish Moses from Joshua. For example, Moses leads a fearful, unprovisioned multitude in silence through the Red Sea. Joshua leads a well-organized, well-provisioned procession across the Jordan, accompanied by a fanfare of trumpets (a detail Origen adds to the scriptural text). Other illustrations of Joshua's greater status and achievements follow. The overall effect of these comparisons is to illuminate the ascending logic of the divine economy. The movement from Moses to Joshua figures the movement from Law to New Covenant; it is a type that discloses how God is lifting up his people to a spiritual worship in which the bounty of the Promised Land is a purified soul. In fact, for Origen the type is not only recapitulated in Jesus, it is reenacted in the life of each believer: "It is similar to when you left Egypt. You crossed the Red Sea, you followed Moses by observing the precepts and the commandments of the law, but here it is that Jesus pulled you back to Moses for a 'second circumcision.' "[13] Thus, the type illuminates the meaning of the book of Joshua, the larger purpose of God in Jesus Christ, and the spiritual ascent of each soul toward the promised land of heaven.

Typology and Christian Practice

Origen's shift from the Joshua/Jesus link to a connection between Joshua/Jesus and the spiritual lives of believers indicates a second important use of typology in early Christian interpretation. Typologies were not limited to efforts to see Old Testament figures as anticipations of Christ. Typologies were also used to connect a variety of Christian practices to the events narrated in the Old Testament. The stories in the book of Exodus provided a rich resource for the church fathers. Just as the Passover lamb was sacrificed to prevent the angel of death from striking the first born of Israel, so the lamb of God died to rescue doomed humanity. The deliverance of Israel serves as a type for the deliverance of all humanity from sin and death.

It is important to recognize, however, that early Christians did not read the Bible so abstractly. Strictly speaking "the deliverance of all humanity from sin and death" cannot function as a primary element in typological exegesis. Typology links event to event, person to person, sequence to sequence. Patristic interpreters maintained a high degree of discipline in their exegesis, developing typologies in which the patterns remain the focus rather than being absorbed into theological abstractions. We must always remember the premodern character of patristic exegesis. Thus, the fathers focused the typological reading of Exodus on developing a link, not between Exodus (discrete sequence) and New Life (theological abstraction), but between the Exodus narrative and the practice of baptism. Just as God had saved Israel from slavery to the Egyptians and delivered her to the new life of the Promised Land by means of the waters of the Red Sea, so God was now saving the new Christian from slavery to sin and death and offering new life in Christ by means of the waters of baptism. Theological ideas are not absent. In both cases divine initiative and redemptive purpose are presupposed. However, as is the case in all typological exegesis, the power of the interpretation stems from the immediacy of the link. The sequence of events in Egypt are connected to the sequence of events that occur when a person is baptized, without the interposition of theological abstractions or generalizations.[14]

A passage from the *Mystagogical Catechesis* of Cyril of Jerusalem illustrates how typology illuminates through the immediacy of association. Cyril explains the sacrament of baptism in three catechetical homilies. The audience is a group of those recently baptized. Cyril draws upon a wealth of material in order to illuminate the significance of the ritual, but the backbone of his explanation is an extended typology. Cyril recalls the actual sequence of events that make up the baptism ritual: "First you entered the antechamber of the baptistery and faced towards the west. On the command to stretch out your hand, you renounced Satan as though he were there in person." He then turns to typology to explain: "This moment, you should know, is prefigured in ancient history." The ancient history is the story of Exodus, which he summarizes: "When that tyrannous and cruel despot, Pharaoh, was oppressing the noble, free-spirited Hebrew nation, God sent Moses to deliver them from the hard slavery imposed upon them by the Egyptians. The doorposts were anointed with the blood of a lamb that the destroyer might pass over the houses signed with the blood; so the Jews were miraculously liberated. After their liberation the enemy gave chase, and, on seeing the sea part miraculously before them, still continued in hot pursuit, only to be instantaneously overwhelmed and engulfed in the Red Sea."[15]

With this sequence in mind, Cyril directs the attention of the newly baptized to what they have just experienced.

> Pass, pray, from the old to the new, from the figure to the reality. There Moses sent by God to Egypt; here Christ sent from the Father into the world. Moses' mission was to lead out from Egypt a persecuted people; Christ's, to rescue all the people of

the world who were under the tyranny of sin. There the blood of a lamb was the charm against the destroyer; here, the blood of the unspotted Lamb, Jesus Christ, is appointed your inviolable sanctuary against demons. Pharaoh pursued that people of old right into the sea; this outrageous spirit, the impudent author of all evil, followed you, each one, up to the very verge of the saving streams. That other tyrant is engulfed and drowned in the Red Sea; this one is destroyed in the saving water.[16]

Those listening to Cyril are encouraged to see themselves as participants in the type. Their confession of faith in Jesus Christ, a confession they have made as part of the ritual of baptism, is portrayed by Cyril as a Christological restatement of the Exodus narrative. Their immersion in the water repeats the Israelite's passage of the Red Sea. The elements of Exodus and Christian faith and practice are aligned to establish a close fit. Both follow the same type. It is as if Cyril were describing the "lock" of Exodus into which the "key" of baptism fits.

This particular typology appears in dozens of patristic texts across the entire period of early Christianity, and it continues to be used in liturgies of baptism and the Easter Vigil. We want to emphasize that Cyril does not presume a causal link between the event of Christian baptism in fourth-century Jerusalem and the event of the ancient Exodus of the sort modern history seeks. Cyril neither believes nor suggests that those who follow Jesus Christ are baptized *because* of Pharaoh's oppression or Moses' leadership. There is no historical economy of influence operating across the surfaces of events. Instead, Cyril's interpretation depends upon the assumptions that Irenaeus articulated. There is a divine economy that orders history from within according to a coherent logic. God saves according to a plan, and what he has done for the ancient Israelites prefigures what he does for those baptized in the name of Jesus Christ. Thus, Cyril's typological interpretation shows that baptism is the new Exodus into the church, which is the new Israel. Both take place within the same divine economy that unfolds according to a common or similar type.

Cyril's explanations of baptism do not rest content with the Exodus/baptism link. He is even more concerned to show how the ritual of baptism follows the type of Christ himself. Cyril teaches that the newly baptized are baptized into Christ. As a result, not only does each person who is immersed in water pass through the deliverance prefigured in the passage of the Israelites through the Red Sea, but, in that same ritual act, each person follows the pattern of the death and resurrection of Christ. Before immersion, each person is stripped of his or her tunic, "in this way also imitating Christ, who was naked on the cross."[17] Each person is immersed three times in the baptismal pool, "therein mystically signifying Christ's three days' burial."[18] In the details of the ritual, the sequence of Exodus is repeated, but the sequence of Christ's saving death and resurrection is repeated as well. Thus, just as Origen moves from a Joshua/ Jesus link to a more complex typological structure in which the pattern of each person's salvation is figured according to the pattern that emerges from the exegesis, Cyril moves from a simple Exodus/baptism link to a more complex Exodus/Christ/baptism typology.

In this typological structure, Cyril follows Irenaeus' exegetical theory. Jesus Christ is the crucial, recapitulating figure, and for that reason he discloses the logic of the divine economy and functions as the hub of interpretation around which the other figures revolve. Indeed, insofar as the church fathers treat interpretation of the scriptural texts as the privileged means for understanding all of reality, Jesus Christ functions as the hub of all reality. This is quite clear when Cyril observes that the events that constitute the death and resurrection of Christ are *more* real than the sacrament of baptism. "The strange, the extraordinary, thing is that we did not really die, nor were we really buried or really crucified; nor did we really rise again: this was figurative and symbolic; yet our salvation is real. Christ's crucifixion was real, His burial was real, and His resurrection was real; and all these He has freely made ours, that by sharing His sufferings in a symbolic enactment we may really and truly gain salvation."[19] Thus, while Exodus might prefigure baptism, for Cyril, baptism "postfigures" Jesus Christ. For the fathers, events that occur after Christ are shaped by him just as events that occur before are similarly shaped.

In order to specify the central role of Christ in the discernment of typological connections, the fathers adopted the technical term *antitypos*. This term has a confusing variety of uses in ancient literature. It occurs twice in the New Testament, once in Hebrews 9:24, where the meaning seems to blend back into the general sense of *typos,* and another time in 1 Peter 3:21. The meaning of antitype in 1 Peter is the one adopted by the fathers. In that context, Christ is presented as the central or disclosing type, the pattern of redemptive suffering that organizes and clarifies our understanding of Old Testament prefigurations and our current experiences or "postfigurations." The church fathers describe this central role as antitypical, drawing on the sense of "in the place of" or "replacing" that is the primary meaning of the prefix *anti*. Thus, for the fathers, to call Christ the antitype identifies him as the master type in which all other types, whether before or after, find their fulfillment.[20]

Cyril's typological analysis of baptism clarifies that Christ's role as "end" or "summing up" should not be understood as a claim about a time sequence. For the church fathers, the historical sequence of human events stretches from the days of creation to the consummating day of judgment. Christ does not end or sum up that sequence by stopping the forward movement of time. Rather, Christ brings the mystery of the historical passage of time to an end by revealing the intention of the divine economy that governs all things. In other words, to use a Christological term, early Christian readers of the Bible treated Jesus Christ as the divine Logos. To return to our analogy of numerical sequences, for Cyril, Jesus Christ is the "$x + 2$" that tells one how to interpret "2, 4, . . ." (Exodus) and "102, 104, . . ." (baptism). This does not mean that Cyril and the church fathers in general imagined that they knew Jesus Christ as one knows a mathematical formula. The eternal Logos of God is incomprehensible. Nor did they imagine that they could finally or conclusively interpret all sequences within the stream of divinely governed human history. Here the analogy to the mathematical series breaks down. To treat Jesus Christ as the Logos simply entails knowing how to orient interpretation, where to look, and what to expect. For the church fathers, the proper method for typological exegesis is to use the figure of Jesus Christ as the touchstone for discerning and developing the sequences of types. He is the antitype who guides the interpreter toward a coherent account of what God is doing in scripture, in the church, and in the lives of believers.

Christ as Master Type

Early Christian readers of the Bible sought to understand how the history and practices of Israel and of the church fit into a coherent whole under the guiding type of Jesus Christ. History, however, is a personal as well as communal reality. We live across sequences of events and experiences that include ritual moments such as baptism, but they encompass much more. Not surprisingly, the church fathers also used typological methods to interpret their own lives and the lives of those around them. In form, the results closely follow Cyril's explanation of baptism. The church fathers consistently read the life of Jesus Christ into their own lives. Where Joshua prefigures Jesus, the followers of Christ postfigure him.

Two examples suffice to illustrate this point: Ignatius of Antioch and Polycarp of Smyrna are represented as exemplary Christians because their lives bore the imprint or type of Christ. Throughout his extant letters Ignatius of Antioch clearly attempts to interpret his own imprisonment and death in terms of the trial, crucifixion, and resurrection of Jesus. Jesus' suffering is the model for his own, and he wishes to follow the path of the type as literally as possible. In his letter to the Romans, Ignatius famously discourages other Christians whom he worries will attempt to rescue him from the fate that awaits him in Rome. Ignatius writes, "I may not only talk [about martyrdom], but really want it." His concern extends beyond proving his commitment. He wishes to be "proven" a Christian in the way in which fire "proves" gold—by becoming Christlike in his own death. "It is not that I want merely to be called a Christian, but actually to be one. Yes, if I prove to be one, then I can have the name."[21] Clearly, for Ignatius, the narrative of the passion provides the template for understanding his courageous journey to his own demise, and the Christlike shape of his journey reassures him.

Later, in a passage dense with allusion to the New Testament, Ignatius further embeds his own life in the typological pattern provided by Christ himself. "My desire has been crucified and there burns in me no passion for material things," he writes to the Romans. "There is living water in me, which speaks and says inside me, 'come to the Father.' I take no delight in corruptible food or in the dainties of this life." Ignatius has crucified his passions and desires. He is following Christ as one who gives up everything for the sake of the kingdom. However, Ignatius pushes the pattern further. Heading toward Rome and his execution, Ignatius views his future as so figured by Christ that he draws his approaching martyrdom into the imagery of the Eucharistic feast. "What I want is God's bread, which is the flesh of Christ, who came from David's line; and for drink I want his blood: an immortal love feast indeed!"[22] As is true of all functioning typologies, Ignatius need not spend time offering explanations. He evokes them as antitypes and himself as the type.

A more extended example of this form of typology appears in the early Christian text known as *The Martyrdom of Polycarp*. The story purports to recount the last days of Polycarp, bishop of Smyrna. Although the text does not make explicit the typological interpretation of Polycarp's martyrdom, any reader who knows the basic gospel accounts of Jesus' death can discern the implicit links. Polycarp's final days are meticulously mapped using the narrative details of the life of Christ. Polycarp is captured away from the city on a farm remarkably like a garden; he is betrayed to the Romans; he submits to his arrest without resistance; he enters the city on a donkey; he refuses to deny his faith before his interrogators. The Roman proconsul is an unenthusiastic persecutor and would like to secure Polycarp's release, but the crowd calls for his death. He willingly submits, and his death seals his faithfulness. Although Polycarp is burned at the stake rather than crucified, many details of his end follow carefully those of Christ's passion.

Although it is unlikely that the Christians who heard this story would have needed it, the author drives home the typology: "We worship [Christ], but we love the martyrs as disciples and imitators of the Lord . . . because of their unsurpassable devotion to their own king and teacher. May it be also our lot to be their companions and fellow disciples!"[23] Just as Ignatius sees himself as being formed by persecution and suffering into a "postfigured" image of Christ, the author of the *Martyrdom of Polycarp* uses Jesus Christ as the antitype. Polycarp and other exemplary followers of Jesus proclaim in their martyrdom the truth of the gospel because they are stamped with the antitype of the crucified savior.

Typology and Economy

Despite our efforts to explain the logic of the patristic use of typology, many contemporary readers of the Bible may still find themselves anxious about a methodology that so cavalierly disregards historical context. Seeking to conform one's life to the figure of Christ, interpreting the practices of the church in the light of their ancient prefigurement, and discerning the person of Jesus in the visages of long-dead ancient heroes may be fascinating to those interested in the history of interpretation, but it has, one might argue, little bearing upon current exegetical practices. When we cast our gaze upon the impressive monuments of patristic typology, are we not engaged more in an act of literary tourism than in one of intellectual and practical formation? Despite the ubiquitous presence of typological associations in our own experience, we may still be inclined to pronounce typology a crippled exegetical practice. Patristic typologies are clever, but are not the fathers, in the end, no different from Star Trek fans who go to conventions where they construct whole patterns of living by moving in and out of a fictional world through acts of intratextual linking? However creative this may be, the world of Star Trek is not a real world, and the meaning generated through the exegesis of that world, however real and helpful for the life of the interpreter, will always be rooted in fantasy. Rhetorical typologies like King's reference to the mountaintop may be poignant and even edifying, but they are decidedly not good exegesis.

We understand these objections; they reflect legitimate concerns about the nature of truth and the plausibility of Christian revelation. However, we are also convinced that when they are inserted into discussion of patristic exegesis they confuse rather than illuminate the issues. It simply makes no sense to say that patristic exegesis was defective because it embraced typological reading. The sheer ubiquity of typological association in human experience argues against such a claim. When contemporary readers object to patristic typology, we are convinced that the true target of their objection is not typology itself but the presumed divine economy across which patristic typology functioned. In other words, the objections are theological rather than methodological.

Earlier in this chapter the figure of Jan Brady's teenage angst helped to illuminate the pervasive presence of typological associations in the interpretation of our experiences. One might argue that understanding the conflict between teenage daughters at the beginning of the twenty-first century in the light of the experience of a fictional character in a 1970s television show is arbitrary and anachronistic. To make an accurate interpretation would we not need to fill in the missing historical details about 1970s suburbia? Would not our reading of the events be improved if we took the time to find out about the director's intentions or, if we are truly fortunate, to gain some clue into the true thinking of the actor Eve Plumb, who played the character of Jan? Such suggestions seem ridiculous because they are ridiculous. The typological connection between Jan and contemporary teenage girls depends upon none of these things. It depends instead on the reliability of the "economy of teenage girls." If we can presume a certain continuity of human experience between teenage girls of the 1970s and teenage girls today, then the typology Jan/teenage girl will function well.

This example may seem too silly to be worthy of serious consideration, but it reveals an important truth about how all acts of typological interpretation depend upon some presumptive connective tissue or "economy." Even modern criticism, for all its claims to objectivity, cannot escape. Consider, for example, historical-Jesus scholar Marcus Borg. In his popular book *Jesus: A New Vision,* Borg presents a thoroughly modern reading of Jesus against the background of certain assumptions about the relationship of spirit and culture.[24] Borg appears to be motivated by a desire to reinvigorate historical-Jesus scholarship with a deeper religiosity without reasserting a traditional pious vision of Jesus that he believes is defective. Because "mainstream biblical scholarship," writes Borg, "has not generated a persuasive alternative image of the historical Jesus," the popular image of Jesus continues to dominate the Christian imagination. Borg would like to offer a more compelling alternative.[25]

Borg's new vision of Jesus unfolds within a particular economy. We might call it the economy of spirit transforming culture. He is eager to reestablish a religious grounding for his interpretation of Jesus, in the wake of what he considers to be the spiritless interpretations offered by much contemporary scholarship. However, the particular form of his vision reflects key convictions of contemporary theology. According to Borg, Jesus participated in the economy of spirit transforming world. He "had an intensely vivid relationship to the world of Spirit, to that 'other reality' sometimes spoken of as the sacred, or the holy, or the other world, or simply as God."[26] One hears echoes in Borg of Rudolph Otto's *mysterium tremendum* and Eliade's ideas about *the sacred*.[27] Borg even indulges in a bit of antimodernism, arguing that because our culture is closed to the spirit world, we experience the power of that world less vividly.[28] Thus, for Borg, both religiously and exegetically we should think in terms of the religious reality that he presumes to exist.

Within this economy of spirit transforming world two antitypes emerge. The first is that of the spirit-filled man who fully brings the spiritual into the world, overcoming our materialism. For Borg the spirit does not affirm the world, the religious economy is not static. It is oriented toward the transformation of society. Thus a second antitype emerges, that of a social critic who challenges conventional wisdom and attempts to revitalize religious institutions and prophesy against unjust practices.

The two antitypes, the spirit-filled man and the social critic, are not evident in the scriptures in any literal or obvious way. They must be drawn out of the text through exegesis. The only way Borg can connect his ideal spiritual personalities to the Bible is to turn to typology. There is no other way to bring the historical particularity of scripture into his economy of the spirit in a transformative relationship to the world. The key for Borg is to show through his exegesis how Jesus actually fulfills the antitypes of spirit-filled man and social critic. As Borg explains, Jesus "radically criticized [his culture], warned it of the historical consequences of its present path, and sought its transformation in accord with an alternative vision."[29] Or again, "a person of Spirit, [Jesus] sought the transformation of his own social world."[30] Jesus, according to Borg, embodies perfectly the basic dynamic of his religious economy, fulfilling both antitypes. By doing so, Jesus becomes a person that we can follow with a new vision, freed from the older distorting image of popular piety. For Borg this means that Jesus' "life powerfully suggests that the Spirit is 'real'" and "Jesus is a model for the Christian life," understood to have a heavy emphasis on social action and countercultural resistance.[31]

We do not wish to decide whether Borg or the fathers have the best perspective on the historical Jesus. We do wish to show that Borg's interpretation of the gospels relies upon type and fulfillment, and this strongly suggests that modern exegetical projects, no less than their ancient counterparts, need this technique to bring the disparate data of the scriptures into a coherent economy. However, to say that both the fathers and modern exegetes like Borg use typologies does not mean that they say the same things. The differences are real. Borg spends no time building typological connections between Joshua and Jesus, he makes no effort to link current sacramental practice to prefiguring events in the Pentateuch, and he does not try to press the pattern of his own life into the mold of the Jesus who emerges in the literal expression of the New Testament witness.

This lack of interest in the typological unity of the Old Testament and Christian practice indicates the key difference. The fathers believed that Jesus was the disclosing antitype. In Borg's case the spirit-filled man and the social critic are the antitypes, and Jesus' religious significance flows from the fact that he embodies these types. In short, the world of the fathers and the world of Borg presume very different economies. For the fathers Jesus Christ is the logos of the economy, to use Irenaeus' term, the *hypothesis* of the scriptures. For most modern theological readers the logos of the economy is something much more abstract. In Borg's view, it is a phenomenological principle of spirit transforming the world. As a result, most modern exegetes who seek to show the contemporary significance of Christ presume typological interpretations that fit Jesus into a pattern rather than establish Jesus as the pattern. To anticipate the next chapter, Jesus is an allegory for Borg's theology of spirit transforming culture rather than the antitype within the divine economy.

While we are sympathetic to patristic sensibilities, we recognize the problems associated with the premodern views, and we have no plans to recommend an uncritical reappropriation of ancient exegesis. Nevertheless, we hope that we have successfully shown that there is nothing arbitrary or anachronistic about the patristic use of typology as it functioned within the ancient divine economy that the fathers took for granted. The economy of Christ was as real and as totalizing for them as various modern economies of historical or spiritual experience are for us. When the fathers connected the person of Joshua with Jesus and the events of the Exodus with baptism, they did so not because they were tragically unschooled in historical method but because they saw these persons and events as in fact connected in the divine economy.

We have largely lost what the fathers had. The divine economy centered in Christ that governed all patristic reading has become dysfunctional. We simply do not believe that "Christ is the end of the Law and the Prophets," at least not in the direct and transparent way that the fathers did. We recoil when we read their biblical commentaries, all of which presume this economy. We allow that adolescent girls might exhibit a true and genuine psychological type of the sort exemplified in Jan Brady, but we have trouble accepting the crossing of the Red Sea as connected in reality to the death of Jesus and Christian baptism. We regard it as present and real only in the imagination of the interpreter. Again, we may be tempted to blame our recoiling on the method itself, but, if we are honest, we recognize that our reaction comes from our profound lack of confidence in the patristic understanding of the divine economy. We have confidence that there exists an "economy of adolescent development" by which we can interpret individual behavior according to type, but we have no such confidence in the economy of salvation in Christ presumed by the fathers as the background for interpretation by type.

One modern author, in an essay attempting to reconcile patristic typology with modern exegetical practice, draws attention to the underlying theological reason why we reject patristic typological interpretation. "The unity of the Bible ought never to mean the same thing for us as for the pre-critical generations," he writes. Instead, expressing the historical-critical sensibility of most modern readers, he continues, the true meaning of the Bible "must be sought in a collection of literature recognized to belong to very diverse times and circumstances, not in a single harmonious body of revealed truth expressing in its complex pattern of interlocking themes, typological, allegorical, parabolic and prophetic, the one vast theme of the divine plan of creation and redemption."[32]

Clearly for this author the essential problem with patristic exegesis is not method per se; the difficulty rests in the defective and obsolete myth of the divine economy. The old Irenaean view that there is a Christ-centered structure that organizes all biblical revelation has been replaced by the post-Enlightenment dogma that revelation is embedded in the events of history shaped by sociological, psychological, and generically religious forces. Thus this critic of patristic exegesis correctly identifies the crux of the matter. We assume an economy of historical and cultural development that is purely this-worldly. The fathers had faith in a divine economy in which, as we saw in Cyril's affirmation, Jesus Christ's life, death, and resurrection is strangely more real, more interpretively powerful, than our own this-worldly lives and experiences.

CHAPTER FIVE

Allegorical Interpretation

The rising of the sun had made everything look so different—all colors and shadows were changed—that for a moment they did not seem the important thing. Then they did. The Stone Table was broken in two places by a great crack that ran down it from end to end; and there was no Aslan.

C. S. LEWIS, *The Lion, the Witch, and the Wardrobe*

In the history of exegesis there is perhaps no term more controversial than *allegory*. Some think allegory a betrayal of the reality of texts, an abuse of the literal sense, and a symptom of an otherworldly aspiration that is disloyal to the world.[1] For these critics, allegory seems a fanciful dance in the ethereal realms of literary imagination. Others think allegory an invitation to expansive vision, an opportunity to unpack the spiritual density of a narrative and do justice to the many layers of meaning that attend all human affairs. Allegory, for its proponents, is not a flight from the literal sense; it is a spiritually enriched and transformed loyalty.[2]

In Greek the word *allegoria* means literally "other speak," and therein lies its controversy. Allegories are basically interpretations that claim that the plain or obvious sense of a given text is not the true meaning, or at least not the full meaning. The words, events, and characters, so the allegorist claims, stand for something else; they speak for another reality, another realm of meaning. The trick, then, is to decode the true or extended meaning and translate the literal sense into its allegorical sense. Or, to change metaphors, allegorical interpretation reads a text as a map. The ordered reality of the text exists not for its own sake but for the sake of guiding our thoughts onto the topography of something else, something more real and more important.

Because allegory is a form of reading that focuses on codes and figures, it is similar to typology. Allegory and typology are part of the same family of reading strategies, often referred to by the fathers as "spiritual," that seek to interpret the scriptures in terms of the divine economy. The difference lies in the amount of work the reader must put into the interpretation. For a well-functioning typological interpretation, two figures are brought into association, and the interpretation convinces (or not) by virtue of the perceived fit. Martin Luther King, for example, appealed to the figure of Moses, and he did so without a supporting infrastructure of explanation. It was sufficient for him to say "I have been to the mountaintop," and those listening to his speech conjured in their minds the figure of Moses. The Exodus narrative came into an illuminating relationship to the civil rights movement. In contrast, an allegory is nearly always a more intentional, explicit, and, for its critics, strained development of association. Unlike typologies, allegories require significantly more interpretive investment capital. The reader must outline the reality for which the text is a map, explaining the coding system of the text so that the message can be read. For this reason, an allegorical interpretation often seems a reading laid *over* the text rather than a reading *in* the text. The interpreter presupposes that the allegorical meaning is not evident in the literal sense, and therefore, the reader must strain to see it.

Allegory involves so much interpretive ambition that it can create the impression that the real source of meaning is in the reader's imagination and not in the text itself. Because the church fathers were committed to the divine authority of scripture, they felt the need to justify their use of allegory. The canonical justification for the patristic use of allegory is found in Galatians 4:21–26. There, Paul turns to the story of the two sons of Abraham as told in Genesis. Ishmael, he reminds the Galatians, was the son of Hagar, Abraham's slave, and he was born "according to the flesh," that is, according to the ordinary ways of sexual desire, fertility, and insemination. Isaac was the son of Abraham's wife, Sarah, a free woman, and he was born by divine grace in fulfillment of the promise that God had made to Abraham. Of the story of Abraham's two sons, Paul says, "Now this is an allegory," and he begins to map Ishmael and Isaac onto his real concerns: the controversy over whether circumcision and other ritual laws of Judaism should continue to define the Christian community. Hagar, he says, represents Mount Sinai and corresponds to the earthly

Jerusalem where the slavery of Jewish law continues to hold sway. Sarah, Paul says, corresponds to the heavenly Jerusalem, where the followers of Jesus have been set free from bondage to the law of circumcision. In short, Paul develops a reading of the story of Hagar and Sarah and their sons as a map of the divine economy of redemption: first, a carnal covenant of slavery (the precepts delivered to Moses) and then, in fulfillment of the promise, a spiritual covenant of freedom (faith in Christ).

Allegories are not only religious in nature. We encounter allegory in our everyday experience in many ways that are not specifically religious. Movies often encourage us to develop allegorical interpretations. J. R. R. Tolkien said his epic trilogy *The Lord of the Rings* was not an allegory. He wanted to protect the story from being translated into something else. Yet, in that story, we are tempted to think of the Mines of Moria through which the Fellowship of the Ring must pass as having allegorical significance. The Mines were developed by dwarves who fatefully dug too deeply and awakened the evil force of Balrog. Are we fanciful when we turn from the literal sense to a different level of meaning and speculate that the dwarves represent modern human beings, and the mines our vast technological enterprise, and the Balrog the horror of nuclear weapons that our relentless digging into the mysteries of matter has awakened? This turn is based upon the narrative structure, location, and characters of the narrative, but it is allegorical. The episode in *The Lord of the Rings* serves as a coded account of the dangers of modern technology, or so our interpretation suggests.

Some of the most influential figures in modern thought have trafficked in allegory. Sigmund Freud developed a theory of psychosexual development that involved a stage in which male children sought to kill their fathers and sleep with their mothers. To dramatize this dynamic, Freud called it the Oedipal complex, suggesting an allegorical interpretation of the Greek myth of Oedipus. The story of the young man who unknowingly kills his father and marries his mother, and thus brings a curse upon his city and himself is not, by Freud's reading, structured by the logic of hubris (the interpretation suggested by Sophocles' play *Oedipus Rex*). Instead, Freud sees a latent meaning that corresponds to the deeper, universal dynamics of the human psyche. Like Paul's allegory, the details of the story of Oedipus serve as a map for an inward economy, in this case not an economy of redemption, but an economy of ego development.

In order to organize our approach to the patristic use of allegory, we propose to distinguish between three basic uses of this interpretive strategy. First, allegories can help make sense of texts that seem to make no sense at the literal level.

Here, the literal narrative is absurd and the text requires allegorical reading to make any sense at all. George Orwell's *Animal Farm* is a good example. In its literal sense, the story concerns animals who have revolted against their human masters and who attempt to create a new "animals' paradise." As readers, however, we do not wonder about the possibility of talking animals who have very humanlike personalities. Instead, we easily fall into an allegorical mode of reading and interpret the story of the animals and their revolution as mapping the dynamics of the Russian Revolution. This is the easiest and least controversial use of allegory, for the impossibility of the literal sense invites the reader to suppose that the purposes of the narrative lie at a different level of meaning.

In many cases, however, allegorical readings do not question or doubt the cogency of the literal sense. Instead, the interpreters press the literal sense to draw out additional meaning. Our interpretation of the Mines of Moria episode in *The Lord of the Rings* is an example. A Freudian reading of *Oedipus Rex* is another. In both cases, the narrative makes good literal sense but contains additional meaning. The interpretation does not doubt or question the literal sense; instead, the reader sees a surplus within the literal sense, and the interpretation is designed to draw it out. Thus, one film critic argues that the movie *Casablanca* can be viewed as an allegory of modern life. "Viewing the film as allegory, each of the characters and events represents a significant aspect of modern life," the critic writes. Adopting the allegorical approach, the movie can serve as a window onto broader themes. "By experiencing this classic film as a modern allegory," the critic continues, "important truths become apparent."[3] One can view *Casablanca* and enjoy the story, but the critic wants us to see more.

Finally, in the third style, allegory can be used to negate the literal sense and redirect the reader's attention. In this style of allegorical interpretation, the literal sense leads in a direction that the interpreter would prefer not to go. This use of allegory nearly always occurs within traditions that vest certain texts with authority. We can read *Animal Farm* if we wish, but we need not. If we find the conceit of talking animals childish, then we can simply set the book aside. This is not the case for religious traditions. Sacred texts are required reading, and interpreters often develop allegories in order to protect the authority of odd or anomalous scriptures.[4] For example, many Christian readers find the genocidal account of the entry of the Israelites into the Promised Land in Joshua troublesome. How does this fit with the divine economy of redemption? The solution is allegory. The land of Canaan is the soul, dominated by the devil; the conquering army is the array of spiritual disciplines endorsed by the church; the goal of the conquest is to set up a kingdom of righteousness in the believer. With an allegorical interpretation, the episode is preserved as sacred in significance.

An interpretive move that directs attention away from the literal sense is, of course, a dangerous game. Allegorical readings, especially of obscure or offensive texts, are prone to spin out of control. The reader can too easily take the text as an occasion to change the subject, with the text acting as little more than a springboard for speculation. Not surprisingly, the history of Christian exegesis has been marked by warnings against and resistance to allegory. However, as we hope to show, patristic use of allegory had a centripetal rather than centrifugal force; it tended toward rather than away from the literal ambience of scripture. Even in the case of troublesome aspects of scripture, the goal was to preserve the sacred significance of the text. For the fathers, allegorical reading was a way of discerning the spiritual depth of the received, authoritative scriptures. Just as they were convinced that the scriptures were divinely structured to sustain typological correspondences, they also presumed that the divine inspiration of scripture gave a spiritual dynamism to the literal sense. The scriptures were the divinely ordained means for entering into the mysteries of salvation, and for this reason, the fathers assumed that the words, episodes, and images of scripture must have an "other speaking" power, an allegorical sense that could direct the reader from worldly realities to the heavenly reality.

Allegory as Making Sense of Nonsense

Consider for a moment the popular song "American Pie," written by Don McLean (Warner Brothers Music, 1971). The song, at a literal level, makes no sense as a narrative. Certainly the words and sentences are in grammatical English, but the references are episodic and seemingly unconnected. The song opens with rather innocuous lines.

A long long time ago,
I can still remember how
That music used to make me smile,
And I knew that if I had my chance,
I could make those people dance,
And maybe they'd be happy for a while.

Quickly, however, the narrative begins to lose cohesion.

But February made me shiver,

With every paper I delivered.

Bad news on the doorstep,

I could not take one more step.

I can't remember if I cried

When I read about his widowed bride,

But something touched me deep inside,

The day the music died.

Who, we begin to wonder is "he" and what is "the music"? What is the "bad news"? Who is the "widowed bride"? As the song progresses, images become odder and increasingly disconnected. We encounter a "jester in a coat borrowed from James Dean," "sergeants playing a marching tune," "Satan laughing with delight," and a "girl who sang the blues." In short, the song makes no literal sense. It seems written in a secret code.

A quick search of the Internet for the occurrence of the words *American Pie* will produce dozens of websites dedicated to revealing the inner coherence of the song. All of these approaches are allegorical. In order to access the "true meaning," one must understand the secret code. In the case of "American Pie," the general consensus seems to be that "the music" is Buddy Holly, "the day the music died" is a reference to his death in Clear Lake, Iowa, in 1959, and the various images in the song are references to the rock-and-roll scene in the decade that followed. This understanding allows for a straightforward set of correspondences. The jester is Bob Dylan. The sergeants are the Beatles. Satan laughing points to the Rolling Stones. Janis Joplin is the blues-singing girl. Once the "real world" of the song is identified, the map of images can guide us into the history of rock-and-roll.

Interpreters of the song "American Pie" need allegory because of the obscurity in the literal text, and that obscurity was the direct intention of the songwriter, designed to prompt listeners to plot out the correspondences. In patristic readings of the Bible, allegory is often prompted by a similar sense of the incoherence of the literal text. Narrative anomalies and inconsistencies in the Bible vexed many patristic readers. We saw, for example, the way in which Gregory of Nyssa, in his *Life of Moses,* was perplexed by the Urim and Thummim that Exodus 28 describes as elements of the priestly garments of Aaron. What could they mean? They seem even more obscure than the "jester" and "sergeants" in the song "American Pie." At a literal level they are obscure, so

Gregory develops an allegorical interpretation in which the literal description of Aaron's priestly garments map out the topography of ascetic practice.

There are countless instances of the same turn to allegory in the patristic tradition that are similarly motivated by the obscurity of the literal sense. One of the key places where Christian thinkers noted problems with the narrative's literal cohesion was in the beginning of Genesis. On the first day of creation, Genesis portrays God creating light, then, on the fourth day, God creates the sun, moon, and stars. This presents obvious problems. How for example, can there be light before there is a sun and a moon? In fact, how can there even be days at all without the rising and setting of the sun? Origen describes this problem clearly in his treatise *On First Principles.* "What man of intelligence," he writes, "will believe that the first and second and the third day, and the evening and the morning existed without the sun and moon and the stars? And that the first day, if we may so call it, was even without a heaven?"[5] In its literal sense, as a sequence of days of the sort we experience, the biblical account of the days of creation would seem impossible to sustain.

Origen was not the only patristic reader to see the anomaly. Some of the greatest ancient interpreters of the Bible clearly identified problems posed by the account of creation in Genesis. For example, in his *Literal Commentary on Genesis,* St. Augustine dwells on numerous difficulties with the literal sense. He points out that there is no universal day and night, as the account suggests. When he affirms the teachings of Genesis, Augustine worries, "I fear that I will be laughed at by those who have scientific knowledge of these matters and by those who recognize the facts of the case." This is because he recognizes that "at the time when night is with us, the sun is illuminating with its presence those parts of the world through which it returns from the place of its setting to that of its rising. Hence it is that for the whole twenty-four hours of the sun's circuit there is always day in one place and night in another."[6] A similar problem holds for the difficulty of reconciling the presence of light on the first day without the existence of the sources of light (sun, moon, and stars) until the fourth day.[7] In both cases, the literal sense will not work on its own; it seems to demand a different approach.

For Augustine, the solution is allegorical. The light of the first day indicates spiritual truth, and its creation on the first day points to the initial and primary creation of intellectual life that is to be illuminated by spiritual truth.[8] This eliminates the problem of light without a sun or moon, for they are the sources of literal or bodily light, and their placement later in the sequence of creation on the fourth day signifies the subordinate status of the literal or bodily realities in the divinely ordained scheme. Moreover, the reference to day and night on the first day is to be understood spiritually. Where Genesis 1:4–5 tells that God separated the light from the darkness and called the light day and the darkness night, according to Augustine, we are not to founder on the literal sense. The night of the first day signifies our spiritual fall into sin, while the morning signifies our renewal and restoration in and through the light of spiritual truth.[9] Thus, Augustine reads the odd problems of light and sun, day and night, in the creation account as pushing the reader toward the standard patristic narrative of creation, fall, and redemption, which is contained *in nuce* in the first verses of Genesis.

Similar concerns about textual ambiguity can be seen in Gregory of Nyssa's famous work *On the Making of Man*. Gregory observes that the book of Genesis presents two separate accounts of the creation of human beings. Genesis 1:27 portrays God directly creating human beings in his own image and likeness. Genesis 2:7 says that God formed Adam out of the dust of the earth, and then, in a later verse, depicts the subsequent creation of Eve from Adam's rib. Contemporary biblical scholars use source criticism to explain the inconsistency, arguing that Genesis derives from two oral traditions. This is not Gregory's approach. He sees the double account as placed in the text to signal the need for a nonliteral, spiritual interpretation. Like Don McLean, who made "American Pie" obscure in order to force us to look more deeply into the history of rock-and-roll, and in so doing adopt an implicit narrative of decline in the music of the 1960s, Gregory views the literal obscurities of scripture as an inducement toward the adoption of a theologically governed view of the human person. The first creation represents spiritual existence, while the second denotes physical or bodily existence. The dual form of the Genesis account is, then, a map by which the reader is directed toward the dual structure of life.

According to Gregory, the first story of creation refers to the creation of human nature as such.[10] It is, if you will, the creation of the form or the archetype of humanity. Gregory focuses on how Genesis 1:27 links God and humanity—"God created man in his image and likeness; in the divine image he created him." This link cannot be physical, for God is a purely spiritual being. Gregory thus concludes that the rational and spiritual nature of God is reflected in the rational and spiritual nature of humanity. This is the primary meaning of Genesis 1:27. Gregory feels justified in reading the text this way because of the ambiguities in the Hebrew word *adam,* which can be rendered as *man* or as the name Adam, depending on the context. In the Septuagint, verse 1:27 is translated with the word *anthropos* (man) rather than the name Adam. The Greek *anthropos* has strong ideal connotations and does not necessarily suggest a particular male person but humanity as such. This adds to Gregory's conviction that Genesis 1 describes the creation of human nature in an abstract or ideal sense, rather than the creation of the individual man Adam. The rational nature of human existence is what is created in the image and likeness of God.

Gregory finds this interpretation reinforced by the rest of verse 1:27—"male and female he created them." He reads this text against the backdrop of Galatians 3:28—"there is neither Jew nor Greek, there is neither slave nor free, there is not male and female." For Gregory, Paul's insistence that, spiritually speaking, there is no male nor female in Christ, warrants a similar approach to Genesis 1:27. The reference to male and female at this point in Genesis, then, does not designate two individuals but rather the dual possibility of male and female within the singular category of rational creatures. As Gregory explains, maleness and femaleness are potential forms of the original rational and intelligent nature; their actual existence is a result of our human embodiment.[11]

Allegorical interpretations are always risky, not the least because the literal sense of texts can be recalcitrant. The first account of the creation of humanity does not just mention male and female; it also includes the commandment to be fruitful and multiply (Genesis 1:28). Here, Gregory must do the kind of maneuvering that often makes allegories complex and unwieldy. He interprets the commandment to be fruitful and multiply as anticipatory rather than directed, in a literal sense, to the first creation of rational existence. It signals God's foreknowledge of the fall and the divine provision to allow human beings to multiply in their postlapsarian state. Thus, from this verse, we do not learn what God might have said to the original couple. Instead, "we learn [that] the irrational is a provision for reproduction." The realities of embodiment and sexual desire—the irrational domain of human existence—are foreshadowed.

By interpreting the first account of the creation of humanity in this way Gregory is then able to turn to the second creation story and show how it completes the larger picture of the human condition. Genesis 2:7 says that "the Lord God formed man from the dust of the ground." Here, the meaning is literal. God has created rational nature in the first episode. Now, God is creating the body in which the rational nature takes concrete form. The dust signals the physical reality of our bodies, to be reinforced by the creation of Eve from the rib or body of Adam. Thus, the second account can be harmonized with the first. The story of the rational creation of humanity, complicated by the narrative's anticipation of the body's future irrational sexual desires, moves to the story of the creation of bodily life, a provision for fallen human nature. In this way, Gregory takes the difficulties of the text to be an allegory for the common patristic assumption that human existence, like the created order itself, is a hierarchical reality in which the spiritual is above the corporeal.

This allegorical interpretation not only conforms to the two-level anthropology and cosmology of the patristic tradition, it also helps Gregory sustain doctrinal claims against alternative accounts of the human condition. Passages in *On the Making of Man* indicate that some of Gregory's opponents thought that God first made Adam's body out of the earth and then breathed life into him. This sequence from dust to breath suggests that the bodily is prior to the spiritual. Such a view conflicts with the basic way in which Gregory understood human affairs. The spiritual is primary, and bodily existence is significant only insofar as it seeks and serves our rational existence as the image and likeness of God. Thus, for Gregory, the allegorical approach establishes the priority of the spiritual nature of human beings over their bodily existence.

The other alternative account of human existence that worried Gregory had the opposite danger. Views associated with Origen speculated about the preexistence of souls that migrated into the body at a later point, as punishment for their sins. This view treated embodiment in such a negative fashion that it cast doubt on the dominant theme of the first chapter of Genesis: that the finite, physical world created by God is good. Because Gregory's allegorical interpretation translates the sequence of the two creation accounts out of the narrative voice of the literal sense and places them into the metaphysical framework of a two-level anthropology, a reading that supports theories of the migration of souls can be resisted. The distinction between the two moments of creation in Genesis is not temporal. God does not first create rational natures and then, later in time, create embodied existence. Both soul and body are created at that same time. For Gregory, the two accounts are not literally sequential. The sequence is allegorical, placed in the text by divine wisdom to guide readers toward an accurate map of human nature; the rational nature of human beings takes priority over the irrational desires of the body.

Augustine's and Gregory's allegories are both structured by a two-tiered vision of reality. Genesis' puzzling claims about light and darkness, day and night, are interpreted by Augustine as referring to spiritual light and darkness on the one hand (the first day of creation), and physical light and darkness on the other (the fourth day of creation). In Gregory's reading, the first account of the creation of humanity teaches us about our rational natures, while the second account depicts bodily existence. Here we encounter a common feature of patristic allegory and indeed all extensive uses of allegory. The allegorical interpretation treats the literal sense as a map by which to navigate into the reality for which the text is an "other speak." Augustine and Gregory adopt the dominant spirit/body geography of antiquity and assume that this geography is the reality for which the confusing portions of the Genesis account of creation were ordained by God to serve as a map. The important point, however, is that neither is neglecting or dismissing the literal structure of Genesis. What they are turning away from is the literal meaning, not the order and sequence of the words. This is especially clear in the case of Gregory. His reading tries to follow the structure of the two accounts of the creation of humanity in Genesis not only to support a distinction between spirit (intellect) and body but also to guide the reader toward the correct understanding of the relationship between these two levels of reality. We need the map in order to guard against false turns and dead ends.

Allegory Adding to the Sense

The second common form of allegorical reading adds a level of meaning that surpasses and completes the literal. C. S. Lewis' famous *Chronicles of Narnia* is representative. These stories relate the literal tale of a magical land called Narnia and the adventures that four human children have there. The narrative in all seven books is perfectly coherent and can be read as the story of the magical land of Narnia. As parents who have read these books to their children know, this is exactly how children receive them. If you happen to be a Christian, however, the *Chronicles of Narnia* can easily seem to correspond to the basic narrative of the fall and redemption of humanity in Jesus Christ. It is natural, then, to develop a second level of meaning to complement the literal. Aslan the lion, who comes to liberate Narnia from the power of the White Witch, corresponds to the King of Kings, who becomes incarnate in order to deliver humanity from the reign of sin and death. For allegorical readers, both levels of meaning are really there. The second, allegorical, meaning is not imposed upon the text; it flows outward from the text.

Those familiar with the Jesuit educational tradition will recognize the term

magis. Latin for "more," the term denotes an important feature of the spirituality of St. Ignatius of Loyola as interpreted by contemporary Christians inspired by his witness. *Magis* refers to going beyond the basics, to seeing the fullness of God's will, and to following with ever-greater commitment the promptings of one's heart to probe the depths of God's love and call. It is, in short, an invitation to go deeper or, in the words of the Gospel, to "come higher" (Luke 14:16). Allegories pursued within coherent narratives are seeking *magis.* When readers of the *Chronicles of Narnia* suddenly realize that the life of Aslan the lion follows the pattern of Christ, they have engaged in allegorical reading that wishes to ascend, to respond to the text's call to "come higher." Allegorical interpretation is not used to illuminate a literal text that makes no sense; in this case, the allegorical reading seeks the *magis* latent in the literal text.

In a similar way, the fathers believed the literal meaning of scripture had the potential to suggest a further, spiritual meaning. We have already seen in chapter 1 how Gregory of Nyssa tells the story of Moses' life on two levels. The first level is the *historia,* the literal meaning that he thinks is perfectly cogent on its own terms. Moses was born a slave in Egypt, he was raised in Pharaoh's house, he fled Egypt, married, saw the burning bush, returned to Egypt as God's instrument of liberation, and died within sight of the promised land. For Gregory, this first level also supports a second, spiritual level that he calls the *theoria* of the text. The literal story is the surface of a mystery. In his account of the *theoria,* he moves from episode to episode in the literal depictions of Moses' life, treating them as a map for the journey of the soul to God. "Those things which we have learned from the literal history of the man we have retraced in summary for you," Gregory tells his readers in the transition to the allegorical sense. "Now we must adapt the life which we have called to mind to the aim we have proposed for our study so that we might gain some benefit for the virtuous life from the things mentioned."[12] Like an astronomer who discovers a new galaxy and focuses his telescope to probe more deeply, the literal events of Moses' life invite Gregory to a deeper analysis.

The *theoria,* then, does not function as an alternative or rival to the text. Gregory is content with the biblical account of Moses' life—so much so that modern readers find him hopelessly naïve in his trust of the historical accuracy of the biblical material—but he is also eager to draw out the spiritual level of meaning. His allegorical interpretation of Moses' life supplements and extends the literal sense by establishing its correspondence to the life of faith. The purpose of the allegorical reading is to transform a canonical story into a narrative applicable to Christian practice. He wants to affect the same sense of *magis* that occurs when a reader of the *Chronicles of Narnia* pushes beyond the literal sense to understand that Aslan's death is about salvation.

Gregory's treatment of the story of the burning bush illustrates how the interpretation supplements and extends the narrative. The episode is, at the literal level, an account of a theophany to Moses, but for Gregory it is also more. As Gregory explains, "That light [of the burning bush] teaches us what we must do to stand within the rays of the true light: Sandaled feet cannot ascend that height where the light of truth is seen, but the dead and earthly covering of skins, which was placed around our nature at the beginning when we were found naked because of disobedience to the divine will, must be removed from the feet of the soul."[13] Gregory is linking the narrative of the burning bush to his understanding of the human condition. Relying on Genesis 3:21, where God is depicted as making "garments of skin" with which to cover the fallen Adam and Eve, Gregory interprets the sandals or "coverings of skin" as a code phrase for the body of sinful desires that clothe our lives. Thus, Gregory's allegorical interpretation of the narrative of Moses shows us that our carnal desires make it difficult for us to correctly perceive God. Sandaled feet cannot ascend. Therefore, we can dwell in the rays of divine light only if we adopt the spiritual disciplines that tear away the hindering "coverings" of carnal desires that shroud the inner beauty of our rational souls.

Gregory's discussion of the plague of frogs follows an identical pattern. The frogs are "ugly and noisy amphibians," and they stink. Contemplating the frogs brings insight into consequences of sinful desire. One sees in the frogs "the sordid and licentious life . . . which, through imitation of the irrational, remains in a form of life neither altogether human nor frog. Being man by nature and becoming a beast by passion, this kind of person exhibits an amphibious form of life ambiguous in nature."[14] For Gregory, sin cannot efface our rational nature. Sin perverts us and turns us into a misbegotten monstrosity of reason in the service of impulse. If the lesson from the frogs is not enough, the plague against the first-born lays down "the principle that it is necessary to destroy utterly the first birth of evil." Only the disciplines of the ascetic life offer hope of escape from the Egyptian slavery to the powers of evil.

In another episode, Moses' departure from Egypt maps the human condition and its journey out of the mire of sin. Exodus 12:11 explains how those preparing for the first Passover should dress: "This is how you are to eat it: with your loins girt, sandals on your feet and your staff in hand, you shall eat like those who are in flight." Gregory turns this into a reflection on the ascetic life. "So that the thorns of this life (the thorns would be sins) may not hurt our naked and unprotected feet," he writes, "let us cover them with shoes." The shoes are not, however, protective covering. "The shoes are the self-controlled and austere life which breaks and crushes the points of the thorns and prevents sin from slipping inside unnoticed."[15] We must put on the protective covering of virtue in order to persevere amid the temptations that assail the way of faith.

Some scholars think that allegorical reading is primarily an act of textual decoding according to a set scheme. Gregory does assume a code, but it is important to see that his reading follows the narrative and not a preestablished system of symbolic meanings. In Gregory's allegorical interpretation, the words themselves do not have univocal meanings. Moses' sandals can signify the body of sin that hides the rational beauty of the soul, as they do in the episode of the burning bush. However, the sandals of the Israelites correspond to the protective habits of self-discipline with which we are to be clothed. The allegorical meaning of sandals shifts because Gregory is following the movement of Exodus from slavery to liberation, which is itself a narrative form of the movement of the divine economy from fall to redemption. Moses' sandals occur in the time of slavery, while the Passover sandals occur in the transition to redemption. The allegorical meaning shifts accordingly. The text maps a journey, and the reading must be following its guidance rather than mechanically adhering to a static scheme of decoding.

Gregory continues with an allegorical interpretation of the clothing God commands the Israelites to wear in preparation for the Passover. "A tunic flowing down over the feet and reaching the soles would be a hindrance to anyone who would diligently finish the divine course." For Gregory the tunic is the clothing of worldly habits. "The tunic accordingly would be seen as the full enjoyment of the pursuits of this life, which prudent reason, like a traveler's belt, draws in as tightly as possible."[16] The path from sin to righteousness must be characterized by discipline. Gregory endorses the severe asceticism of his time. Those who seek the face of God should be always ready to tighten the belt of self-restraint. As Gregory rounds out his interpretation of the clothes for Passover, he notes that "the staff for repelling animals is the message of hope, by which we support the weariness of the soul and ward off what threatens us."[17] The way of self-discipline cannot be sustained unless one trusts in the promises of the gospel and dwells in the hope of everlasting life.

We could continue at some length detailing Gregory's allegorical interpretation of the life of Moses, but we have seen enough to illustrate the point. In this case allegorical reading functions as a superadded *magis* that runs on a parallel course through the literal details of the narrative. The allegorical interpretation does not refute or deny the literal sense, nor does it attempt subversion; it simply adds more and does so according to the narrative structure. Gregory's shifting interpretation of the significance of sandals is an especially clear instance in which patristic reading, even in its push toward the allegorical meaning of scripture, remains tied to the text. In this way, the allegorical reading strives to press the details of the narrative into the service of Christian practice. The life of Moses is not just a biography; his sandals are not just coverings for his feet. His life can be read as a map for every Christian engaged in the ascetic pursuit of virtue.

Saving the Sense with Allegory

Finally, allegories can be prompted when the literal meaning of a text is seen to run in a wrong or unhelpful direction. In this instance, the reader is unhappy with the literal meaning, and the allegory tends to replace rather than supplement. This use of allegory was common in antiquity. Neoplatonic philosophers frequently applied allegorical techniques to the interpretation of Homer. Like early Christianity, Neoplatonic philosophy endorsed severe asceticism that grew out of a two-tiered view of spirit and body. The true home of the human spirit was to be found in the timeless, unchanging, and eternal realm of truth, and the philosophical life required lifting the mind from thoughts about worldly, bodily realities to the contemplation of truth. The raw sensuality of Homer's epic poems would seem to offer little to a Neoplatonist bent on highlighting the glories of the intelligible realm. The duplicity and sexual rapacity of the gods in the *Iliad* present an obvious embarrassment. At a more subtle level, the *Iliad* and *Odyssey* portray worldly honor as the greatest goals for men, undermining the otherworldly ideals of Neoplatonism. Yet, the Hellenistic tradition held the Homeric epics in great esteem. As a consequence, there emerged an allegorical tradition of reading that directed attention away from the literal atmosphere of the poems and toward the teachings of Neoplatonic philosophy. The culturally authoritative texts were affirmed, but under the guidance of allegory.[18]

Portions of the Old Testament can have a similar disconcerting effect. In the world of patristic exegesis, a devotion to the inspired truth of scripture did not prevent the fathers from turning away from the literal sense. The most famous example is the Song of Songs. Early Christian interpreters recognized the sexual overtones of this book, and the patristic consensus (which corresponded to the Jewish consensus of their time) was that the salacious literal sense of the Song of Songs is inconsistent with the principles of pious interpretation. The sensuality that oozes from the text is at cross purposes with the severe asceticism that the church fathers endorsed. Yet, because it was scripture and inescapably sacred, the text had to be read. The solution, then, was to adopt an allegorical interpretation that focused on the soul's love for God and the divine matrimony of Christ to the church. The allegorical strategy directed attention away from the erotic literal sense and toward a spiritual sense that conformed to patristic conceptions of the larger scheme of salvation.

Origen offers a thoroughly redirecting allegorical interpretation of Song of Songs. At the opening of his commentary he notes the special character of the text and acknowledges its literal sense: "It seems to me that this little book is an epithalamium, that is to say, a marriage-song, which Solomon wrote in the form of a drama and sang under the figure of the Bride, about to wed." Modern scholarship rejects the traditional assumption that Solomon was the author of the Song of Songs, but Origen's basic characterization of the literal sense is uncontroversial. For Origen, the love or marriage song should not be read according to its literal sense. Instead, the sensuality and passion needs to be transformed from that of the carnal world to the spiritual realm. In Origen's account, the bride is "burning with heavenly love towards her Bridegroom, who is the Word of God. And deeply indeed did she love him, whether we take her as the soul made in his image, or as the Church."[19] For Origen, then, the bride is the soul or the church, the bridegroom is the Word of God, and the passionate imagery of physical desire is the longing of the soul or church to fulfill the promise of redemptive matrimony that Paul suggests in Ephesians 5:32.

With this allegorical scheme for the text, Origen goes on to explain how the highly eroticized images fit nicely within the ascetic project of the Christian life. The passionate imagery of sexual love mutates under Origen's masterful exegetical orchestration into the imagery of a spiritual passion that loves God without the distractions of earthly and created things. Origen stays with the narrative details, but the meaning that emerges has lost all connection to carnal eroticism. A few examples from the early part of the commentary should suffice to illustrate this metamorphosis.

The first line of the Song of Songs begins suggestively, "let him kiss me with the kisses of his mouth." The sexual passion is patent. Origen's allegory, however, redirects the passion. His basic assumption is that the desire and the consummation it seeks requires illumination by the "unadulterated doctrine of Word of God," which the ardent believer experiences in the form of "kisses." These kisses arouse not physically but spiritually and intellectually. They are the kisses of truth. Moreover, Origen is keen to exploit the verbal detail. He draws attention to the excess of love imagery. "The plural 'kisses,' " he writes, "is used in order that we may understand that the lighting up of every obscure meaning is a kiss of the Word of God bestowed on the perfected soul."[20] With this comment the allegorical interpretation circles back upon itself as a self-warranting exercise. To press for deeper interpretation, as Origen does, even interpretation of seemingly unfitting sexually loaded imagery, is to receive ever more "kisses" from the redeeming Word himself.

The next verse begins with equal suggestiveness: "your breasts are better than wine." Here, Origen relies on the associative technique, reading the word *breast* in the light of John 13:23–25 where the beloved disciple rests against the breast of the Lord. Origen then returns to the verse, interpreting it as recommending that the Christian rest in the Word that is better than wine, for the Word is the source of all wisdom. As is the case in Origen's exegesis, no detail passes unexamined. He was eager for the many kisses. In this case, the "wine" represents "the ordinances and teachings" of the Law and the Prophets. This sets up an allegorical recapitulation of the basic patristic account of the relationship between the Old Testament and the New. "Realizing now that the instruction and the knowledge that are to be found in the Bridegroom are of high eminence, and that a much more perfect teaching than that of the ancients issues from his breasts," writes Origen, "the bride (follower of Christ) says: 'your breasts are better than wine'—better, that is to say, than the teaching with which she was gladdened by them that were of old."[21] The covenant on Sinai gave rest and repose to the Israelites, for such was the divine plan, but for Origen, the breast of the Lord gives full and final rest, for he is the fulfillment of the covenant and the source of all wisdom.

Origen relies on more than an associative link between Old and New Testaments based upon the word *breast*. Like all patristic readers, he piles layer upon layer of interpretation. In this case, he develops a typological connection. Origen explains that the pattern of comparative superiority of breast over wine is the same as that which we find in the gospel parable of the treasure hidden in the field (Matt 13:44). The one who sells all to buy the field and the bride who rests on the breast of the bridegroom attest to identical truths within the divine economy. The field is worthy of purchases just as the old covenant is worthy of Christian loyalty. However, like the breasts that are better than wine, the buried, spiritual treasure supersedes the agricultural, bodily value of the field. Thus Origen concludes, "the breasts of the bridegroom, who is hidden like a treasure in the Law and the Prophets, are better than the wine that those contain—that is to say, the teaching in them that is open and rejoices all who hear."[22]

As a final example, we consider Origen's comments on verse 1:3: "Your name is as ointment emptied out. Therefore have the maidens loved you." Here Origen fixes upon the word *emptied* and hears echoes of Philippians 2, where Christ is said to have emptied himself and taken the form of a slave. He then weaves the Christological structure of Philippians into his account of the verse from the Song of Songs. "For the sake of these young souls, therefore, in their growing and abundant life," Origen writes of the maidens, whom he consistently reads as signifying the followers of Christ, "he who was in the form of God emptied himself, that his name might be as ointment emptied out, that he might no longer dwell only in light unapproachable and abide in the form of God." For Origen the ointment is a sweet perfume. "The word of God was made flesh, and so these maiden souls at the beginning of their progress might not only love him, but might draw him to themselves."[23] The verse of the Song of Songs that in its literal sense speaks of a handsome prince whose reputation makes women swoon is transformed into an allegory that speaks of the incarnation of the Word and how he voluntarily humiliated himself for the sake of these maidens and their illumination and progress in wisdom.[24] It is no wonder that the maidens (all souls who long for God) love him (the incarnate Word) and that, as described later in the verse, they are drawn to him and run after him (with the swift feet of ascetic discipline).

These examples should be sufficient to demonstrate how Origen used allegory to redirect the erotic imagery of the Song of Songs toward a spiritual meaning. When Origen and others interpreted the Song of Songs as an allegory of the soul and the church, they did so precisely because the text was considered scripture. Their allegorical readings did not have the modest goal of making difficult texts innocuous. As we can see very clearly in Origen's assimilation of the love poetry of the Song of Songs to the Christological structure of Christian faith, patristic allegory consistently assumed that scriptural texts were ordained by God as a map for navigating from sin to righteousness. Allegory may mean "other speak," but for the fathers the allegorical sense seems to always speak about the divine economy of redemption, sometimes from the Christological perspective of God's initiative and at other times from the perspective of ascetic human participation. The job of the faithful reader is to work out this "other speak" according to the codes and sequences present in the words and verbal structures of the biblical text.

Allegory and Economy

The persuasiveness of allegorical readings depends very much upon the economy the interpreter presupposes. As we saw in chapter 4, this is true for typological interpretation. The kinds of connections that typology makes between figures will seem persuasive only if one is convinced that they are "real." This confidence comes from the faith that scripture is organized and structured according to a divinely ordained economy. Cyril of Jerusalem can coordinate baptism with the crossing of the Red Sea because he views the whole sweep of biblical history and the Christian life as governed by a single divine intention. Since an allegorical interpretation self-consciously abstracts from the literal sense, it is even more dependent upon the plausibility of the economy that supports the correspondences between the literal and allegorical senses. One must be convinced that Paris exists in order to be confident that reading a map of Paris will be helpful in navigating the twisting streets.

Many contemporary readers think patristic allegorical interpretations are little more than the pious fantasies of the precritical mind. For them, textual obscurity or discomfort ought to be illuminated by history, not schemes of spiritual discipline or anthropologies of spirit and body. A wayward text should challenge our assumptions rather than prompt a counterintuitive rereading, and a text should be allowed to say what it means and no more. For these critics, allegorical reading tends to spin out of control. In their view, attempts to discern the "other speak" of scripture must be resisted and, ultimately, rejected because they are dangerous and wrong.

The influential modern patristic scholar R. P. C. Hanson, in his *Allegory and Event*,[25] argued that allegorical exegesis of the sort practiced by the fathers was unredeemable and illegitimate given the new understanding of interpretation that modern historical-critical study has introduced. Assessing Origen's exegetical legacy, Hanson writes, "at best we might describe [Origen's method] as quaint and sometimes poetical; at the worst it is a device for obscuring the meaning of the Bible . . . [Origen's approach] since the arrival of historical criticism, has had to be entirely abandoned and is, as far as one can prophesy, never again likely to be revived."[26] The meaning of the Bible, in Hanson's view, is what the text meant according to the original author's intention. The task of the exegete is to recover that intentionality using the methods of historical inquiry. For Hanson and others, then, allegory is perverse. It is a flight from history, the real subject matter of the Bible. It treats the Bible as a map for a world of spiritual truths that does not exist—or exists only in the religious ideology of early Christianity.

We do not want to question Hanson's overall claim that patristic allegorical interpretation is a scandal to modern readers whose interpretive assumptions are formed by historical-critical inquiry. The categories of his assessment, however, do not hit the mark. Ironically, when Hanson urges us to seek to discern the original intentionality of the authors of scripture, we observe that the church fathers would agree. Gregory is very confident that his allegorical reading is justified because it seeks the original intention of the author, who is the spirit of God. Still further, when modern critics claim that patristic allegory neglects the texts and does little more than superimpose theological and philosophical ideas upon it, we must point out that Origen's allegorical interpretation of the Song of Songs dwells on verse after verse, word after word. Origen's allegorical approach hardly supports the charge that he is indifferent to the particularity of the text or that he superimposes his reading as one might project a picture onto a blank screen. Origen seeks the allegorical rather than the literal meaning, but in the literal ambiance of the text. One is hard pressed to find many modern commentaries that have such an intensive focus on the literality of the text. The historical critical approach has no reason to dwell on *kisses, breasts,* or *wine.* Origen, in contrast, searches within the words so as to receive the many "kisses" from the mouth of the divine Word. He treats the Song of Songs as a map to guide readers toward a spiritual understanding, but we are false to his exegesis if we do not recognize that he follows the map of the literal sense very closely indeed.

Our responses to some of the standard objections to allegorical interpretation point out the difficulty that modern scholars have understanding just what they find to be so off-putting about patristic exegesis. When modern scholars read Origen's *Commentary on the Song of Songs,* they often feel as though they are being thrust into a strange world of occult meanings. Their heads spin as Origen weaves his interpretation with threads of verbal association, typological insight, and recourse to spiritual practices, guided by his convictions about the centrality of Christ. The result of this dismay is nearly always misdiagnosis. Modern readers tend to say that the problem is the use of allegory as a method for reading. The assumption is that if the fathers had paid attention to the text as texts, they would not have pursued such theologically saturated readings. But is this so? Allegory is not a controversial interpretive strategy because it ignores texts. Again, Origen and Gregory focus on the literal reality of scripture as the crucial locus of the allegorical sense. The controversy stems from their readings' dependence upon the economy that supports the ambition of plotting correspondences between the literal and the "real" meaning. Allegory is uniquely transparent to the presuppositions of the interpreters. In the end the controversy surrounding the practice of allegorical reading really has to do with the superstructure supporting the correspondences, not the intellectual act of making them. Allegorical interpretation offends by what it presumes and not by how it proceeds. A contemporary example illustrates.

In *Begotten Not Made: Conceiving Manhood in Late Antiquity,* Virginia Burrus undertakes an historical study of manhood in the ancient world as seen through the lens of feminist criticism.[27] She allows that the controversies of fourth-century Christianity concerned doctrinal debates about the nature of God and that this involved any number of issues in theology, ascetic practice, and exegesis. For this reason, the standard histories of doctrine are accurate as far as they go. However, because the patriarchal imagery and social system that supported the doctrinal debates are antithetical to her sense of moral and religious truth, Burrus finds the surface meanings of fourth-century Christianity unhelpful, even offensive. Like Origen and the *Song of Songs,* Burrus does not turn away from the history of doctrinal development. She describes herself as having a deep affection for the church fathers, to whom she is bound like a "perversely loving daughter."[28] She is loyal to the history, and she wants to reinterpret and reappropriate the church fathers rather than simply discard them. Like Origen, she wants to redirect the meaning away from the offending sense.

To do so, she proposes a scheme of correspondences in which the patristic vocabulary is decoded and interpreted as having a psychosocial dynamic of both transforming gender identity and reinforcing patriarchal authority. "It is by attending closely to the rhetorical 'flash of swords' in the doctrinal debates of the fourth century," that she hopes to show that "in the late Roman Empire, theological discourse came to constitute a central arena in which manhood was not only tested and proven but also, in the course of events, redefined." Doctrine is not only about doctrine. For her, "when the confession of the full and equal divinity of the Father, Son, and Spirit became for the first time the *sine qua non* of doctrinal orthodoxy, masculinity was conceived anew, in terms that heightened the claims of patriarchal authority while also cutting manhood loose from its traditional fleshly and familial moorings."[29] Thus, Burrus' study has an allegorical structure not unlike a Freudian interpretation of Sophocles' drama *Oedipus Rex*. The fathers are talking about God and salvation at the literal level, but at the allegorical level, they are really talking about gender and authority. We want to unpack Burrus' allegorical interpretation, for it demonstrates the central role of economy—in her case, an economy structured by feminist theory.

Burrus' allegorical interpretation of the church fathers is quite clever and intriguing. Let us look, for example, at her treatment of the passage from Gregory of Nyssa's *Life of Moses* that we considered in the introduction. The episode concerns Moses' "rod," which became a snake and consumed the snakes of the Pharaoh's magicians. Where Gregory moves from one scriptural use of *rod* to another, Burrus exploits the contemporary sense of *rod* as a euphemism for penis. The same holds for the use of the word *snake*. This allows Burrus to develop allegorical correspondences and to read Gregory's discussion as a veiled expression of sexual and gender dynamics. As she writes, "Vanquishing the serpentine forces of a hyper-masculinity, the rod also purifies the man of the swampy mire of a 'frog-like life.' However, when struck against the dry rock that is Christ, the rod 'dissolves hardness into the softness of water,' so that the rock 'flows into those who receive him.' "[30] By her reading, then, the real meaning of Gregory's commentary ranges from male anxiety about competitors with larger penises (serpentine forces), as well as the male desire to plough fallow fields (dry rocks) with their semen, to the ascetic goal of becoming the receptive vessel of divine impregnation rather than the active agent of reproduction (flows into).

A reader positively or negatively responds to Burrus for the same reason that we might accept or reject Origen's interpretations—because of the presumed economy that supports the allegorical reading. Christians find Origen's analysis insightful because they are inclined to think the scripture was written for the edification of the faithful. They suppose, in other words, that there is an economy that shapes scripture so that it teaches a coherent, spiritually valuable meaning. Moreover, while modern Christian readers may not be as enthusiastic as Origen was about the severe asceticism of early Christianity, they are equally inclined to believe that the spiritual meaning of scripture will follow the general pattern of the divine economy revealed in Christ, a pattern that includes transformative self-discipline. The same holds for anyone reading Burrus. Those sympathetic to her reading will easily embrace her use of the literal sense of patristic literature as a map to guide us through the dynamics of patriarchal authority and male identity in early Christianity. The larger acceptance or rejection of Burrus' analysis will not rest on the use of an allegorical method. Instead, decisions about the truth or falsehood of her interpretation of patristic literature will depend, to a great extent, upon whether or not readers think Burrus' assumptions about a feminist economy of personal and social life are true.

The issue is not simply one of expressing preferences for one economy over another. Our "faiths" interact with our interpretations in a mutually reinforcing fashion, making it impossible to distinguish between the organizing assumptions and the material results of interpretation. If we are inclined to think that ancient Christianity was structured by patriarchy, then Burrus' interpretations of Gregory's use of *rod* and *serpent* ring true, not because we are being "ideological" but because we assume that the very idioms and images of the church fathers do *in fact* have a patriarchal logic. If we believe in a feminist psychosocial economy, we will not think she is inventing her allegorical reading. She is uncovering the true meaning of gender and sexual dynamics encoded into the texts by the "intentions" of the social system in which the church fathers were enmeshed. The same holds for Origen. If we are inclined to think that Christ is the incarnate Word of God who fulfills the scriptures, then we will not think Origen's reading "doctrinal." We assume that the very idioms and images of the Song of Songs do *in fact* have a Christological shape. Origen, then, is not inventing his allegorical interpretation. He is uncovering the true, redemptive meaning encoded into the Song of Songs by the divine intention that structures all of scripture (and all creation and history).

We now return to the question posed before the discussion of Burrus. Is methodology really the root cause of modern rejection of patristic allegory? Were one inclined to offer a critique of Burrus, one could take our demonstration of how her analysis follows the allegorical structure of Origen's reading of the Song of Songs and conclude that both are examples of the abusive evils of allegory. We can well imagine Hanson drawing such a conclusion. However, such a critique would not ring true. There is nothing wrong with her method, she only stands out among historians because her aggressively allegorical approach makes the superstructure of feminist historiography more visible. The fact of the superstructure is not notable. Scholars engaged in historical study use larger categories and conceptual frameworks to make sense of the past and its texts. Ernst Troeltsch, an early twentieth-century German theologian and church historian did not use the allegorical method to write his history of the development of Christianity, *The Social Teachings of the Christian Church*.[31] Instead, his more restrained methods were guided by what he took to be a universal economy of religious development. Whether or not one finds these social theories persuasive is not the issue; all historians need to presume an economy of causality and influence that allows them to connect events and organize the data into some meaningful whole. That Burrus analyzes the church fathers guided by the historical assumptions of modern feminism is no more scandalous than interpreting early Christian history guided by a theory of social development from a blander and more widely accepted source. The scandal, if there is one, is in the economy that guides the interpretation, not the strategies of reading, even the allegorical strategy.

Therefore, there are two lasting objections to allegory that highlight the real issues at stake in patristic exegesis. The first objection amounts to an appeal to modesty. As we have said, allegory is a revealing method of interpretation. Our assumptions about the deep structuring principles of reality are visible in the construction of an allegorical interpretation. When we suggest that the reader think of the Mines of Moria episode in *The Lord of the Rings* as an allegory of the thermonuclear dangers of modern science and technology, we are putting our cards on the table. We can easily be mocked as science-phobic humanists. The same holds for Burrus and the church fathers. Her readings of patristic use of words such as *rod* reveal her presumed feminist economy. The way that she reads the patristic map makes no sense unless we assume the reality of gender politics and patriarchy. The allegorical readings of the church fathers made their doctrinal commitments very visible as well. Origen has no reason to associate the sensual *kisses* of the love poem with the "kisses" of the divine word other than the Christian economy of redemption. For many modern scholars, this is unseemly. Better to operate more modestly, where the density of literality provides a thicker fabric for interpretation. Better to work locally and refrain from the synthetic interpretive efforts that must place texts within a larger frame of reference, within an economy.

The second objection is quite simple. In chapter 4, we heard from a modern scholar who saw the deepest problem with patristic interpretation: the church fathers really believed that God governs all things, that human beings have fallen into sin, and that the only begotten Son, who is the Word of God in the creation of all things, becomes incarnate to draw human beings into the divine life and bring the created order to its final perfection. In sum, they believed in the divine economy outlined by Irenaeus. This belief structured their interpretive imaginations in the same way our beliefs in various economies of historical, social, and psychological development shape our interpretive imaginations. Life is short. One cannot look for what *might* be real. One looks for what one thinks really *is* real. So, the church fathers looked for Christ and the ascetic life they thought Christ called us to live in everything, especially in the divinely ordained instrument of Christian revelation, the scriptures. The objection, then, is simply that their faith was a fantasy. Jesus Christ is not the incarnate Word of God. Reality is structured according to mundane laws of nature and the dynamics of cultural, historical development.

We cannot respond to these objections on behalf of the church fathers. We can only report that they did not view interpretive modesty as a theological virtue. They believed that God saturated scripture with a great wealth of truth, and zeal was the right disposition to take as an interpreter. "Seek and you shall find," was a basic hermeneutic principle that they felt with existential force. And what of their belief in the divine economy? We are not foolish enough to try to defend their faith, which they knew to be a divine gift and not a human accomplishment. "Those who have eyes shall see, those who have ears shall hear."

CHAPTER SIX

The Rule of Faith and the Holy Life

> At the first turning of the third stair
> Was a slotted window bellied like the fig's fruit
> And beyond the hawthorn blossom and a pasture scene
> The broadbacked figure drest in blue and green
> Enchanted the maytime with an antique flute.
>
> T. S. ELIOT, *Ash Wednesday*

Vince Lombardi is a great source of athletic wisdom. "In truth," he is reported to have said, "I have never known a successful man who did not appreciate the discipline that it takes to win." Lombardi's observation seems obvious, but the bite of the maxim is less in the speaking than in the implementation. He understood that the requirements of discipline applied equally to the player's skilled application of the rules of football and to his character as a man: both forms of discipline guide toward success. The same holds for the church fathers. They knew that inspiration can deliver insight whenever and to whomever it will, just as some gifted athletes seem able to manage victory without discipline. As Augustine observes at the outset of his treatise on scriptural interpretation, some attain wisdom by the direct action of the Holy Spirit.[1] Nonetheless, just as Vince Lombardi exhorted his players to strive with disciplined effort so also did Augustine and the early Christian tradition as a whole, conceive of the interpretation of scripture as an endeavor best pursued with a similar focused exertion. They found scriptural support ready at hand: A wise child loves discipline (Prov 13:1).

That exegesis was profoundly disciplined may strike many contemporary readers as overstated. Not a few critics of early Christian interpretation have condemned it as an uncontrolled and reckless approach to scripture. Many modern readers think patristic exegesis far from disciplined, an exercise of theological fantasy. Not surprisingly, the most frequently reported transgression is the patristic failure to adequately account for the historical reference of the Bible. For these critics, revelation is found in the historical event; scripture is but the surviving record that scholars must assess and analyze in order to recover, as best they can, actual knowledge of the past. Because the fathers sought to interpret the text as text and not as a culturally saturated window upon the events that really matter, modern readers throw up their hands in exasperation. "The fathers," they say, "naively took the historical accuracy of scripture for granted. Their interpretations move across the surfaces of the Bible. They lack the critical discipline to probe behind the texts to try and discern what really happened."

Apparent methodological incoherence is a second source of vexation to contemporary readers. It is extremely difficult for those who are trained in modern approaches to the Bible to understand why a given patristic interpreter moves from a literal to a typological to an allegorical reading, or why the interpretation might flow in the opposite direction. One modern author is stymied by Irenaeus' approach to Genesis. Within Irenaeus' exegetical digressions in *Against the Heresies,* he observes that "within the space of only a few pages, God's instruction to Adam concerning the fruit in Paradise (Gen 2:16) is interpreted first allegorically —make use of all Scripture, but without pride, or having contact with heretics— and then literally." He then draws a conclusion common for modern readers of patristic exegesis: "It is clear that Irenaeus considered it to be normal that, for certain passages of Scripture, the allegorical sense should be superimposed on the literal one, but he never felt the need to elucidate the ways in which this superimposition of meanings operated." For this author, Irenaeus' failure to explain what he was doing is evidence that Irenaeus had no "clear hermeneutical principle of his own." Because of this he was forced to "resort to the principle of authority" to resist his Gnostic opponents.[2] The conclusion is that patristic exegesis, lacking methodological grounding, is no better than the worst forms of argument from authority.

These reactions to patristic exegesis demonstrate how different their approach was from ours. The fathers did not view history in a modern way, and they did not embrace a modern methodology because they did not hold the modern referential theory of the meaning of scripture that underwrites our

historical-critical disciplines. We tend to think that the Bible is important because of the x that it represents: historical events, ancient religious sensibilities,
ideas, doctrines, and so forth. For this reason, we adopt disciplines that help us
get from the scripture to the x. For example, if we think that the book of
Leviticus represents the taboo system of ancient Israelite religion, then we
might use a sociological theory of taboo to organize our reading of the text. We
discipline our reading in order to bring out what we imagine to be the proper
subject matter of the text. The same holds if we are convinced that the gospel of
Luke reveals the truth about Jesus Christ as a report on the events that occurred.
We then adopt historical methods to weigh the evidence that the story presents, trying to bring what actually happened into focus by screening out the
obvious ways in which the author's faith colors the telling of the story. In each
instance, the exegetical discipline flows from a perceived need to focus and
concentrate attention on the subject matter of the text.

The intellectual disciplines and methods of modern biblical interpretation
are as diverse as the various assumptions about the x that the text is taken to
represent. If one thinks the x is a sequence of historical events, then historical
methods predominate. If one assumes that the x is the religious consciousness
of the ancient writers, then other methods are employed. It is not our intention
to explain modern exegesis. We want to explain the fathers and their approach,
and this requires us to put aside for a moment some of our assumptions about
what might count as disciplined exegesis. We need to see that they focused their
attention differently because they had different assumptions about the subject
matter that required their concentrated attention.

For the fathers, the scriptural text itself is the subject matter of interpretation; it is not the means to that subject matter. Origen is typical. He describes
the study of scripture as a subjection of the mind to the scripture, and in that
subjection, one who ponders the details of the text will find that "his mind and
feelings will be touched by a divine breath and he will recognize that the words
he is reading are not utterances of man but the language of God."[3] The scriptures say exactly what the reader needs to hear, and the disciplines of reading
therefore are not oriented toward using the text to get to some further x. The
scriptures are the x, and the interpreter's job is to adopt the disciplines and
methods suitable to drawing ever closer to the "language of God," for the mind
that conforms to the specificity of the scriptures is shaped in a divine fashion.
To think in and through the scriptures is to have a sanctified vision.

What could it possibly mean to think "in and through the scriptures"? An
analogy to modern science may help. For the scientist, the natural world does

not represent or refer. It simply is the subject matter of inquiry. Indeed, a great deal of early modern science fought to free itself from the theological presupposition that the deepest and most important function of the natural world is to refer to God's benevolence in the act of creation, manifest in the ordered purpose of all things. A parallel rebellion was raised against Aristotelian metaphysics and its analysis of reality in terms of final causes, for in the scholastic theology of premodern Christianity, this analytical tool was crucial for demonstrating how nature points the mind of the observer toward God. Thus, modern science developed methods, not to get beyond or behind the natural world but to see *into* it. An evolutionary biologist wishes to explain fossil data rather than discern or interpret what the data might represent. The data are what matter most; data cannot be a means or medium for something more important. The hallmark of modern science, experimental method, serves this goal. It brings the data into focus as the control upon scientific theory.

The same holds for the fathers. They treated the literal givenness of the scriptures as the deepest and most fundamental data. The scriptures are, to recall Origen's blunt statement at the outset of *On First Principles,* the sole basis for wisdom. One can easily imagine a contemporary scientist uttering a parallel claim that the facts are the sole basis for lasting knowledge of the real world. Of course, unpacking just what it means to say that "the facts" are the basis for science is notoriously difficult. The philosophy of science is a rich and varied discipline because the interaction of scientific theory and experimental data is no clearer than the relationship between Origen's speculative theology and the text of scripture. Nonetheless, the interesting questions and debates concern *how* data controls scientific inquiry; the consensus among scientists is that, however that control might be understood, it exists.

Patristic interpretation is structured and disciplined in much the same way as modern science.[4] Methods such as intensive reading are ways of establishing connections between data points. Figural and allegorical interpretation are strategies for constructing larger interrelationship and bringing various aspects of theory into an intellectually satisfying synthesis. Just as the evolutionary biologist is committed to discerning the meaningful patterns in fossil data and to correlating those patterns with prevailing evolutionary doctrine, the fathers had analogous commitments. A figural association of the Exodus story of the crossing of the Red Sea with the practice of baptism serves to order and organize Christian self-understanding. The same holds for allegory, as we have attempted to show in some detail.

The important point, however, is not to rehearse the ways in which patristic interpreters thought through the specific details of scripture. We want to emphasize the underlying assumption that the church fathers shared. Once one thinks that the scriptures are divinely inspired, then the primary project is not to assess them. There are legitimate questions about the quality of the data. As we have seen, Origen used text-critical tools to clean up what he thought were the corruptions that had made their way into the manuscripts of the Bible. However, Origen saw that his primary job, like that of a scientist, is to interpret data, not to question its reliability. On this point, Origen is representative of the patristic tradition. The church fathers sought to explain how the vast heterogeneity and diversity of scriptural data might be brought into an intellectually satisfying form. This was the basic project of interpretation, as they understood it.

For modern scientists, the job of interpreting data is difficult. It is easy to go wrong, and modern science implicitly adopts Vince Lombardi's view that success flows from discipline. This discipline has two forms that will help us understand the fathers. The first form is communal. A modern scientist is a creature of intense socialization. One may be born with aptitude, but one is not born a practicing scientist. At the outset of scientific training, emphasis falls on doctrine. One must learn the dominant theories in order to participate in scientific inquiry. Thus, rising students are tested on the basis of their knowledge of the dominant theories and how they can be applied to data. The second form of discipline is personal. Objectivity is a scientific virtue. We have strong incentives to form our minds around convenient or reassuring hypotheses, and we need to discipline ourselves to allow what is the case to predominate over what we wish to be the case. For this reason, most science teachers have the tenor of moralists, exhorting their students to adopt and respect the disciplines of the scientific method. Vision must be focused and sharpened, and we have often heard our colleagues refer to their favorite students as "committed to science."

The fathers urged forms of discipline analogous to those we find in modern science. For them, scriptural interpretation was an ongoing research project under the guidance of a body of doctrine that they called the rule of truth or rule of faith. The rule functioned in a fashion similar to modern scientific doctrine, and the aspiring interpreter needed to be socialized into the rule for some of the same reasons. A community of inquiry functions at a sophisticated level when the investigators do not feel the need to constantly reinvent the orienting hypotheses used to motivate questions and formulate answers. Moreover, just as modern science identifies certain virtues as indispensable, so did the fathers link the formation of character with right reading of scripture. Objectivity may not have been the executive virtue of early Christian exegesis as it is for modern science. Nonetheless, just as the modern practice of science requires investigators to discipline their desires for convenience (or fame) because such desires might distort experiments and analysis, the church fathers endorsed a regime of spiritual discipline.

The Discipline of the Rule

The church father most closely associated with the rule of faith is Irenaeus of Lyons. In chapter 2 we discussed how he framed an overall reading of scripture based upon the hypothesis that the diverse layers of biblical material reflect a divine dispensation or economy that is summed up or recapitulated in Jesus Christ. On an intellectual level, this disciplines Irenaeus' reading of scripture. To assume a hypothesis is to adopt a stance that focuses and constrains assumptions, allowing one to organize material and offer an account of how the many individual pieces fit together. Our concern, at this point, is not to rehearse Irenaeus' articulation and use of the hypothesis that Jesus Christ is the fulfillment of the scriptures. We are more interested in what Irenaeus says about how he acquired the hypothesis, for these observations provide insight into the ways in which patristic interpreters understood the disciplining role of doctrine.

For Irenaeus, the scriptures should be read according to the "rule of truth" or, as it is often called elsewhere in the patristic tradition, the "rule of faith." Irenaeus never gives a definitive statement of the rule. His references to the rule of truth often involve differing formulations that can frustrate a historian searching for a precise definition. In some instances, the way in which Irenaeus states the rule seems to point to subsequent creedal affirmations of the doctrine of the Trinity. The rule specifies, he reports, "the faith in one God the Father Almighty, Creator of heaven and earth and the seas and all things that are in them, and in one Jesus Christ, the Son of God, who was incarnate for our salvation, and in the Holy Spirit."[5] However, the content of the rule that Irenaeus endorses cannot be assimilated to the creeds that were later formulated. The rule also includes a summary of "God's dealings and economy," which might fairly be called a synopsis of the basic plot of the biblical narrative from Genesis to Revelation.[6] In still other places, the rule seems to be a simple affirmation of the existence of the divine economy: "We hold to the rule of truth, that there is one God almighty who founded everything through his Word and arranged it and made everything."[7] The specific content of this rule remains elusive. It is a fluid array of doctrines, some involving specific claims about the nature of God in relation to both creation and salvation, and some articulating a narrative scheme that outlines the divine economy.

However difficult to pin down in material content, Irenaeus is clear that his hypothesis for the interpretation of scripture comes from this rule. The rule orders and disciplines his reading, and if we trace Irenaeus' use of the idea of a rule of truth, we can see that it has an intrinsic and extrinsic function. Irenaeus claims that the rule is the principle or logic of scripture itself. It is the right rule to use because it articulates the divine order within scripture. It is the right plan because it describes that actual architecture of the Bible. However, for Irenaeus, the rule is also communally authorized, and he emphasizes this aspect. The interpreter should accept that authority in order to properly frame exegetical questions and discern the right answers. Thus, for Irenaeus, the order of discovery is different from the order of being. Correct interpretation flows from the extrinsically given rule to the discernment of the intrinsic scriptural logic of fulfillment in Christ. One finds the rule in scripture if one accepts its authority from the church.

The key to the intrinsic meaning of the rule of truth is Irenaeus' assumption that the entire Bible admits of a cogent, overall interpretation. Like a giant crossword puzzle, this overall interpretation must be worked out in detail, as he attempts to do in the endless exegetical digressions of his treatise. Of course, Irenaeus does not succeed in working out all the details of scripture and tying up the loose ends. He allows that he "cannot discover explanations of all those things in scripture which are the subject of investigation," and all wise interpreters recognize that "in regard to those things which we investigate in the scriptures . . . , we are able by the grace of God to explain some of them, while we must leave others in the hands of God."[8] An overall reading of scripture is his ideal, not something he attains. However, if we adopt the rule of truth, then we can entertain the details of scripture "with a harmonious adaptation of its members, and without any collision."[9] The rule promises to order our interpretation so that, however impossible might be a complete and final reading of the whole of the divine testimony, "all scripture, which has been given to us by God, shall be found by us perfectly consistent . . . , and the many diversified utterances there shall be heard as one harmonious melody in us."[10] Thus, for Irenaeus, the rule of truth is vindicated by its ability to bring harmony and order to the heterogeneity of the scriptural data. It is a rule that, once adopted, maximizes the ability of the interpreter to offer a cogent reading of scripture taken as a whole.

Here, Irenaeus is working as would a modern scientist. No evolutionary biologist can tie together all the fossil data into a giant crossword puzzle of interlocking evidence. The evidence is too vast and heterogeneous. Instead, biologists examine data and seek to identify patterns. At some point, they gain confidence that the data is following certain patterns, and though there is always more data to consider, a hypothesis is offered. In this sense, the biologists propose a rule of truth suitable for the data under consideration. At one level, of course, the rule is subjective. The biologists are proposing an interpretive approach. Yet, the very reasons for advancing the hypothesis are the patterns the biologists think present in the data. In this sense, the rule of truth is intrinsic. The same holds for Irenaeus. To use his vocabulary, scripture is "the body of truth," and that body functions harmoniously.[11] The body of truth functions according to the laws of its nature, and the rule of truth articulates those laws. Thus, it does not matter how Irenaeus has acquired his initial assumptions about the order and logic of scripture, just as it does not matter if the evolutionary biologists developed their hypothesis on the basis of intuition, the suggestions of a friend, or on the basis of currently existing theory. The rule is the right one to adopt because it allows readers to join the members of the body of scripture into their proper order and connection.[12]

We have attempted to explain three methods of reading adopted by the fathers: intensive, figurative, and allegorical. All three, we have argued, are "data sensitive." They depend upon the discrete particularity of the biblical text. Not surprisingly, then, the fathers emphasize close attention to the verbal, literal reality of the Bible. In his treatise on the proper methods for biblical interpretation, *On Christian Doctrine,* Augustine is clear that one must put in time in the laboratory in order to have something intelligent to say. "He will be the most expert investigator of the Holy Scriptures who has first read all of them and has some knowledge of them."[13] Indeed, for Augustine, as for nearly all premodern interpreters of scripture, knowledge is most secure when the scriptures are committed to memory.[14] One is hardly competent to offer hypotheses about data one does not know, and the more familiar one is with the data, the more likely one is to offer accurate hypotheses. The intensive readings that the fathers undertake, as well as the figural and allegorical patterns they discern, arise as a result of this familiarity with the verbal, literal reality of scripture. The sudden shifts from one part of the Bible to another that we often find in patristic exegesis occur because the fathers have a great deal of the Bible memorized. To move from a verse in Genesis to a word in Proverbs and its echoes in the gospel of John, as do the fathers, reflects an intimacy with the details of the scriptural text, and when the church fathers provide exegetical comments that jump from place to place in scripture, we should not think of their practice as arbitrary. They are gathering data from diverse locations in the Bible, just as an evolutionary biologist might pull together diverse sources of fossil data in order to establish some patterns in the evidence.

As modern readers, we are aware that the fathers fashion their readings according to preconceived ideas about just what the Bible, as a whole, teaches. In this sense, they do not "find" the rule of truth in the text. The rule is extrinsic. It is something brought to the material. However, we need to beware imagining that this is unique to patristic exegesis. We see the same construction of a rule of truth in all forms of intellectual inquiry. Modern scientists often talk of the laws of nature, but in their more reflective moments, they admit that they teach their students hypotheses, not laws. The evolutionary biologist is proposing an interpretation of the data, not reading a law off the data as one might read out of a textbook. The hypothesis is laid over the data to see if it will fit. It is necessarily extrinsic to the data, resident in the mind of the investigator as a strategy for bringing order to the evidence.

Irenaeus affirms that the rule of truth is applied to the scriptural text as a framework for reading. It structures the reader's attention and determines how to organize the material. In chapter 2, we discussed Irenaeus' analogy of the mosaic. Irenaeus' basic claim against his adversaries is that the Gnostic interpreters approach scripture with a schematic plan for the mosaic that causes them to create the wrong picture, and in so doing, they must deform or modify the various pieces that were created in order to be put together to form the image of a handsome king. Irenaeus does not imagine that you or I could pick up the Bible and intuit the right ordering of the pieces into the handsome king. We need to have the right directions or rule beforehand. If we know how the pieces are supposed to go together, then we greatly increase the likelihood that we will make correct exegetical decisions about the details.

Augustine gives a clear analysis of the rule of faith as the orienting basis for analyzing difficult passages. He observes that we often face tough decisions about punctuation and orthography in the manuscripts of the Bible. (Ancient manuscripts did not have punctuation or capitalization.) In chapter 3, we saw how Origen employed ancient strategies of textual criticism to see if he could resolve difficulties by comparing manuscripts and translations. Augustine was not a textual and linguistic scholar like Origen, but he also urged that interpreters gain knowledge of Hebrew and Greek (though he did not know those languages himself!). This knowledge allows readers to check translations and clear up linguistic puzzles. However, not all difficulties can be solved in this fashion, and in such cases, the rule of faith provides guidance. "When investigation reveals uncertainty over how a locution should be pointed or construed," Augustine writes, "the rule of faith should be consulted as it is found in the more open places of the scriptures and in the authority of the church."[15]

The example Augustine gives is the punctuation for the first verse of the gospel of John. He tells us that we can read the verse in two ways: "In the beginning was the Word, and the Word was with God, and God was," or "And the Word was God, the same was in the beginning with God." No aspect of the manuscripts or original Greek will settle this question, for the punctuation must be interpreted into the verses by the reader according to the sense he wishes to give. Should we read John 1:1 as affirming that the incarnate Word was created by God in the beginning to do his work? This interpretation would seem permitted by the unpunctuated text, and as we saw in the discussion of Athanasius in chapter 3, it is the Arian reading that follows Proverbs 8:22: "The LORD created me at the beginning of his work." For Augustine, interpretation is not an isolated intellectual undertaking. It takes place under the guidance of the rule of faith. Therefore, he concludes that the Arian reading of the punctuation "is to be refuted according to the rule of faith which teaches us the equality of the Trinity."[16] The rule functions to settle the right way to handle an uncertain passage, just as evolutionary theory would serve to tip the scales one way or another when a scientist is trying to interpret a novel or obscure piece of data.

For Augustine, the orienting role of the rule of faith also guides the reader toward the proper use of either a literal or figural interpretation of various parts of scripture. Here, Augustine anticipates a modern worry about patristic exegesis. We tend to think that the church fathers switch back and forth from literal to figural or allegorical forms of reading without any methodological control. Augustine would seem equally worried. As he puts the problem, "We must beware not to take figurative or transferred expressions as though they were literal," and we must also be careful "lest we wish to take literal expressions as though they were figurative." The proper guard against this twin danger, for Augustine, rests in adopting the proper method or path of interpretation. "Generally speaking," writes Augustine, "it is this: anything in divine discourse that cannot be related to either good morals or to the true faith should be taken as figurative."[17] In other words, the discipline of the rule of faith, which for Augustine has a behavioral as well as doctrinal component, guides. It serves as the method for controlled reading.

When modern readers encounter this definition of proper method, they are taken aback, but they should not be. The analogy in modern science is patent. When a scientist must decide which data are primary (to be taken "literally") and which are anomalous (to be taken "figuratively"), the decision is most often made on the basis of existing theory. The experimental method *produces* data. It cannot interpret it. In the act of interpretation, the scientist asks what is consistent with the prevailing scientific consensus ("good morals") and existing theory ("the true faith"). The difference, of course, is that what is judged anomalous in science is often discarded, and when it cannot be discarded, something like a figurative interpretation is offered. Scientists explain how the data are not "real" but are results of poorly designed experiments. Or, in still other cases, they develop an explanatory theory that argues, in essence, that the data only *appears* anomalous. The history of science has many examples of "figurative interpretation" of data. The Copernican theory of epicycles in circular planetary rotation may be seen as a figurative form of data analysis. Tossing out difficult and puzzling verses of the Bible is not an option for Augustine, nor can he try to explain away passages as defective. Because he takes the scriptures to be the word of God, all the data is "good data." Therefore, more plastic techniques of figurative and allegorical interpretation must be applied.

Any large-scale interpretive project, whether of diverse fossil data or diverse scriptural material, requires an initial, rule-governed approach by which the details might be brought into the proper order. The question of *how* we form our hypotheses therefore becomes very important. Mistaken assumptions and ill-conceived rules lead us into dead-ends and force us to manhandle the data to make it fit. Given the bad consequences of adopting ill-conceived doctrines, we are wise to consider just what we accept and from whom. Irenaeus addresses this concern directly and frequently. He is very clear that his own hypothesis stems from the doctrine taught to him by an earlier generation of faithful witnesses to the rule of truth. "We have learned from none others the plan of our salvation," he writes on behalf of all orthodox readers of scripture, "than from those through whom the Gospel has come down to us."[18] Irenaeus takes the apostolic origins of the rule of truth to be a decisive source of its authority. He places a great deal of emphasis upon the succession or continuity of those who teach the rule in their roles as bishops of the churches founded during the time of the apostles.

Like all participants in sophisticated intellectual projects, Irenaeus is appealing to a tradition of interpretation, a tradition that has a settled body of doctrine just as modern science has a settled body of theory. He takes that tradition to make a rightful claim upon the interpretive imagination of scriptural readers because it is venerable and because it has a proven track record among the leaders of the church. A reader who does not adopt the rule of truth, Irenaeus argues, "would always be inquiring but never finding, because he has rejected the very method of discovery."[19] Adopting the rule of faith sets the reader down the right path; it offers an appropriate method by which to control interpretation.

Irenaeus is likely wrong about his assumptions about the structure and governance of the Christian communities in the decades immediately following the time of Christ, and he may be rashly generalizing from his own experiences in Asia Minor. His rule of truth may not have had such a continuous and widespread history. Moreover, Irenaeus may be materially wrong about the interpretive fittingness of the rule he has been taught, whatever its source, just as Ptolemaic astronomers who promoted the geocentric theory of the solar system were wrong. Nonetheless, on the formal point Irenaeus is surely correct. An ordered and structured theoretical framework is necessary for the interpretation of complex and diverse sets of data. Unless we begin with focused questions and organization of the data according to established principles, we have as much hope of providing a plausible interpretation of the scriptures as a young student who forsakes introductory classes in physics has of saying anything sophisticated about the laws of planetary motion.

The Bible surely is a complex and diverse set of data, and the rule of faith Irenaeus so tirelessly promotes functions as an ordered framework for interpretation.[20] Sophisticated interpretive approaches, whether in science or in other disciplines, require communities or schools of collective, cooperative effort in order to inculcate, develop, and sustain their research programs. No well-developed train of thought can emerge, *ex nihilo*, out of the minds of individuals, no matter how brilliant they may be. Thus, while Irenaeus' appeal to a communally mandated rule is certainly based upon religious assumptions about its apostolic origins, it also reflects the inevitable conditions for a large-scale, all-things-considered interpretation of something so massively detailed and diverse as the Bible.

Because Irenaeus ascribes apostolic authority to his teachers and the rule they taught him, we should not assume too much similarity between patristic interpretation and modern science. A scientist does not give such great authority to the provenance of a theory or the antiquity of a seat of learning, and there is no scientific virtue in maintaining continuity with past teaching. Nonetheless, we should beware of accentuating the differences too much. In the first place, modern science does function as a continuous tradition of inquiry that provides current investigators with a body of doctrine that is presumed to be a reliable guide to the interpretation of difficult and novel data. One receives training in modern scientific doctrine and method, and only within the context of this training is one "authorized" for faculty appointments. Like Irenaeus, the explanatory imagination of the modern scientist is communally disciplined. Moreover, even though the authority of the continuous tradition of established leaders of original Christian churches carries far greater weight in Irenaeus' mind than scientific tradition carries for the contemporary scientist, his appeal is not entirely unfamiliar. Irenaeus is rather like a person who refutes a creation scientist by saying that no Harvard biology professors have either believed or taught this form of pseudoscience. This appeal does not settle the question. The authority of established institutions and the consensus of reputable members of an academic discipline are never sufficient to prove or guarantee the truth of any particular theory. Nonetheless, in a public debate, the appeal to authority carries weight.

We have pressed the analogy with modern science in order to explain how the rule of faith disciplined patristic interpretation. Our readers may find this shocking because what they may know about the exegesis of early Christianity is likely framed by the assumption that it was nothing more than an exhaustive exercise in proof-texting animated by an anti-intellectual submission to doctrinal authority. This response is ill informed. We are too likely to imagine that what is different from our own approach is ignorant. The church fathers themselves analyzed the similarities and dissimilarities between ancient versions of scientific inquiry and scriptural interpretation. They came to some of the same conclusions about the disciplining role of the rule of faith that we are suggesting here.

Clement of Alexandria, a learned third-century Christian intellectual who lived in Alexandria, a scientific center in the ancient world, offers reflections on the disciplines proper to philosophical method. "There are certain criteria common to men," Clement explains, "such as the senses; and other [criteria] that belong to those who have employed their wills and energies in what is true—the methods which are pursued by the mind and reason, to distinguish between true and false propositions." Our ideals for scientific inquiry are not the same as the ancient ideals, but the underlying sentiment is similar. Reason must be held accountable. The same need for accountability obtains for biblical interpretation. One cannot approach the scripture without discipline. Yet, for Clement, the methods or rules for reading scripture are not philosophical. One does not approach the divine word with the same methods one might use to determine the movements of the stars. Instead, the discipline comes from the authority of the rule of faith taught by the church. Heresy, reports Clement, stems from a lack of adherence to the rule. "For in consequence of not learning the mysteries of ecclesiastical knowledge, and not having capacity for the grandeur of the truth, too indolent to descend to the bottom of things, reading superficially, they have dismissed the scriptures."[21] Heretics are to Clement as creation scientists are to modern biologists. They refuse the authoritative doctrines and fall into error accordingly. They appeal to the wrong criteria, and the result is a mismanagement of the relevant questions and possible answers.

We might not like the set of rules embraced by the fathers, the overall "take" they adopted in order to pursue a disciplined interpretation of scripture. We may legitimately ask, "Who says that these rules delineate the true vision of Christianity?" We may well adopt a different tradition of interpretation and work out an account of the diversity of scripture in a very different way. We may think the fathers are just like creation scientists, clever but misguided, and we may argue for another body of doctrine, formulated according to the canons of historical method, by which to focus and order interpretation of the Bible. Our purpose is not to defend the truth or falsehood of the rule of faith that came to define the orthodoxy in the early Christian world. We want only to explain how that rule operated as an exegetical control. For if we understand how that rule functioned, then we cannot dismiss the exegesis of the fathers as uncontrolled invention produced without a clear method. The notion that the interpretation of the early church was "subjective" is either trivial or nonsensical. Of course it was subjective in the sense that all intellectual inquiry is contingent upon the effort, imagination, and insight of each individual investigator. Yet, as we hope to have demonstrated, that individual effort was self-consciously constrained by the adoption of a dominant theory of how the scriptural texts fit together, just as modern science is guided by dominant theories in its inquiries. One might call the rule of truth that Irenaeus promoted mistaken or wrongheaded, but it makes as much sense to say he was subjective as to say that Aristotle was subjective just because his accounts of human psychology or the natural world have been discarded.

Spiritual Discipline and Interpretation

We have pressed an analogy between patristic exegesis and modern science. Insofar as early Christian interpretation is an intellectual project, we think the analogy illuminating. Yet the tradition of patristic exegesis, like the religious faith it sought to serve and promote, was much more than an intellectual undertaking. As we have seen, Augustine says that proper interpretation must be guided not only by true faith but also by "good morals." Indeed, to even divide faith and morals would have been unthinkable for the church fathers. Irenaeus criticizes his Gnostic adversaries for failing to adopt his hypothesis for the interpretation of scripture, and he frequently denounces them as engaged in all sorts of immoral behavior. The rule of faith was a rule for life as well as a rule for reading scripture and teaching its meaning. It was a spiritual rule that guided the whole person toward fellowship with God. Not surprisingly, then, the church fathers argued that a reader must have spiritual discipline to control exegesis.

In modest ways, our present academic culture acknowledges the role of personal discipline in the intellectual life. Sloppy thinking stems from laziness and the attractions of easy, convenient, or conventional conclusions; thus, objectivity is a virtue that we must acquire through the discipline of desires. It cannot be learned out of a textbook. Because no one person can be a specialist in all fields, or even in the many subfields that make up the academic disciplines, scholars consistently assess the trustworthiness and judgment of their peers. All the footnotes cannot be checked; all the primary sources cannot be read, and, for this reason, we tend to rely on the virtues of other scholars as much as on our own analysis of the primary material. "Is this or that historian careful or responsible?" This and other questions of character are common.

However significant the role of character might be in the community of scientists, it pales in comparison to the patristic approach. The integral role of spiritual discipline stems from the assumptions that the church fathers made about the subject matter of interpretation. They assumed that the scriptures were divinely inspired. This does not entail any particular theory of divine authorship. Sometimes the church fathers say, "Moses intended such and such" in their exegesis. At other times they say, "the Holy Spirit intended" or "the spirit of prophecy guided," and so forth. In spite of these differences, the patristic tradition was unified in its belief that scripture is saturated with the divine. "The scriptures are indeed perfect," writes Irenaeus in a characteristic exclamation, "since they were spoken by the Word of God and his spirit."[22] The sacred texts do not just provide good data; they are fragrant with the aroma of the redemptive sacrifice of Jesus Christ. Thus Origen wonders, "Who, on reading the revelations made to John, could fail to be amazed at the deep obscurity of the unspeakable mysteries contained therein, which are evident even to him who does not understand what is written? And as for the apostolic epistles, what man who is skilled in literary interpretation would think them to be plain and easily understood, when even in them there are thousands of passages that provide, as if through a window, a narrow opening leading to multitudes of the deepest thoughts?"[23] The goal of patristic exegesis was to pass through the narrow opening that led to thoughts that participated in the unspeakable mysteries, and only a person whose vision has been refined by prayer, fasting, and self-control could hope to effect such a passage. Therefore, the fathers identified interpretive skill with the ambitious regimes of ascetic practice that defined the spiritual endeavor of the ancient church.[24]

Augustine, for example, associates interpretation with the spiritual journey toward God. He likens us to lost travelers, "miserable in our wandering and desiring to end it and to return to our native country."[25] In this lost condition, we "need vehicles for land and sea which could help us to reach our homeland."[26] The whole world of created things, for Augustine, has been ordained by God for our use in return to fellowship with God, our native country. To recall Irenaeus' vocabulary, all things are set up in an economy, a dispensation or order that, if properly engaged, will lead toward Christ and through Christ to the eternal godhead. However, we fail to use all the aids and vehicles to make progress. The problem is not simply intellectual. For Augustine, we take delight in specific aspects of the finite world and become "entangled in a perverse sweetness."[27] Our desire to return to God shifts and turns into a love of finite things for their own sake. As a result, instead of making progress we stagnate or even fall backwards. Out of a love and desire for finite things, writes Augustine, "men are driven back from their country by evil habits as by contrary breezes, seeking things farther back from and inferior to that which they confess to be better and more worthy."[28] Elsewhere, Augustine shifts from sea to land: "We are on a road which is not a road from place to place but a road of affections, which [is] blocked, as if by a thorny hedge, by the malice of our past sins."[29]

For Augustine, the problem is not that we have bodies and live in a world of finite, temporal reality. Sin is not ontological, as if being created rather than uncreated were the original curse. The issue is our relationship to all the changeable, diverse features of the created world. We can either love and enjoy finite reality, taking it to be the sum total of what makes life worth living, or we can use that reality in order to make spiritual progress toward the infinite and eternal truth that is "the Father, the Son, and the Holy Spirit, a single Trinity."[30] The latter is the way of sanctification, for it requires us to discipline our finite loves so that they might come to serve a crowning love of God. This requires a discipline of self-purification. As writes Augustine, "the mind should be cleansed so that it is able to see [the divine light] and cling to it once it is seen. Let us consider this cleansing to be as a journey or voyage home."[31] This cleansing, moreover, is not speculative or abstract. It involves the specific moral and spiritual disciplines of the Christian life or, as Augustine puts it, "good endeavor and good habits."

The scriptures are constituted by words and sentences that participate in the finite world. As Augustine recognizes, to say that the Bible is divinely inspired does not mean that it is divine. The languages are culturally specific. The manuscripts have all the potential for corruption and decay that characterize all bodily existence. The literal sense of the words is circumscribed and particular. Therefore, Augustine is clear that scriptural exegesis requires the same moral and spiritual discipline that our use of all finite things requires. The mind must be cleansed in order to cling to the divine light revealed in scripture. This requires the interpreter to die to worldly loves so as to live as one who loves God with all his heart, all his soul, and all his mind.[32] From this principle, Augustine draws out a spiritual discipline for scriptural interpretation. "Whoever, therefore, thinks that he understands the divine scriptures or any part of them so that it does not build up the double love of God and of our neighbor does not understand it at all."[33] Needless to say, this principle can only be applied if the interpreter already participates in the double love of God and neighbor. Those whose minds are cleansed of the influence of worldly desires and whose lives are immersed in the disciplines and practices of the Christian life participate in this double love. Therefore, "anyone who knows the end of the commandments to be charity"—and, for Augustine, to know something is to participate in it—"he may approach the treatment of [divine scriptures] with security."[34]

Augustine was not unique. The role of sanctity in scriptural interpretation is dramatized by Athanasius' widely circulated account of the great Egyptian monk, Anthony. Athanasius wrote the *Life of Anthony* in order to commend and promote the monastic ideals of severe ascetic discipline. The *Life* describes a series of temptations that Anthony overcame as a young man and the sanctity he achieved, followed by a great number of triumphs made possible by Anthony's holiness. The result is a hagiography, a story that seeks to highlight an ideal of holiness. This is very handy for our purposes because the hagiography of Anthony exemplifies in narrative form Athanasius' vision of spiritual discipline and its role in the life of the church as a whole. One episode in the *Life of Anthony* testifies to Athanasius' conviction that the holiness of one's life is more decisive than learning in the interpretation of scripture.

Athanasius makes it clear to his readers that Anthony was illiterate. Although he had memorized scripture, he was not a scholar who was probing the finer points of doctrine, nor was he ever a student who could have learned the dominant traditions of interpretation. Yet, Athanasius portrays Anthony as possessing great power of discernment. When confronted with heretical teaching, Athanasius writes, "perceiving their wickedness and apostasy from the outset, he never held communion with [them] . . . , for he held and taught that friendship and association with them led to injury and destruction of the soul." If he was illiterate and untutored in theology, how could Anthony have recognized the false teaching? According to Athanasius, Anthony's sanctity provided him with insight into the truths of scripture. Anthony had retreated to the inner mountain of the desert, a symbol of his great achievement as one who has denied himself all worldly things for the sake of devotion to God. From this pinnacle of ascetic perfection, "once when some of [the heretics] came to him, sounding them out and learning that they were impious, he chased them from the mountain, saying that their doctrines were worse than serpents poison."[35] The heretics were false interpreters of scripture, and the illiterate Anthony, educated by his spiritual discipline, could discern their error.

We should beware imagining that the scene described by Athanasius occurred as he describes it, or even that it occurred at all. Athanasius' long life was marked by a violent conflict with rival Christian groups in Alexandria, where he was bishop and from which he was forced, at times, to flee. His battles with these rival groups concerned the relation of the incarnate Logos, Jesus Christ, to the eternal Father and creator of all things. As we saw in chapter 3, that controversy was, at root, a debate about the interpretation of scripture, and Athanasius' great intellect was devoted to mastering the extensive exegetical arguments that he thought demonstrated the truth of his position. One need not adopt a complex critical theory to see that Athanasius was eager to associate the

spiritual heroism of Anthony with his own position against the heretical opponents. What is telling, however, is that Athanasius, the scholar bishop, was
eager to promote Anthony, the illiterate monk, as a great guardian of orthodoxy. The authority of sanctity and ascetic discipline seems to have functioned
in Athanasius' mind (and we might assume in the minds of his readers as well)
as a powerful complement to the subtle arguments of exegesis governed by the
rule of faith.

While Augustine and Athanasius affirm the crucial role of personal sanctity
and spiritual discipline in the project of patristic exegesis, Origen provides the
most extensive and integrated account of just how and why discipline of the
soul must guide the interpretation of scripture. Origen assumed, like all the
church fathers, that the Bible has an obvious, bodily sense that is widely accessible, but it also has another, spiritual sense, "which is hidden from the majority
of readers."[36] It is notoriously difficult to discern just how Origen understood
the relationship between these two levels of scripture. He formulates the relationship between the body or literal sense of scripture and its spiritual sense in
the following way. "The contents of scripture are the outward forms of certain
mysteries and the images of divine things."[37] It is wrong, we think, to conceive
of the "outward forms" as separable from the mysteries they convey. For Origen, scripture is more nearly iconic than symbolic. Nonetheless, we need not
settle this controversial issue in order to see the consequences of this picture of
scripture as an embodied spiritual sense, consequences that Origen draws out
with singular clarity.

Because scripture has a tiered structure of obvious and hidden meaning, the
exegetical project parallels the journey of the soul depicted by Augustine. The
mind of the reader must be properly prepared to engage the obvious, literal
level of scripture so as to discern the spiritual, hidden meaning resident within.
This preparation cannot be merely intellectual. For Origen, the reality of the
human person is threefold: body, soul, and mind. He draws this anthropology
from the Platonic philosophical milieu of his time. The mind is the human
capacity to contemplate God. It denotes our capacity to receive the spiritual
teachings of scripture. The soul is our deliberative capacity that directs us to
follow this or that path of thought or action. The body is the seat of physical
desires and sensations. Origen links this view of the human person to our
journey to God in and through the senses of scripture. To grasp this link, we
need to understand Origen's view of human destiny.

Origen's vocabulary and pattern of thought derives from Platonic philosophy. This clear influence can lead us to think that he recapitulates the Platonic view of the nature and fate of the body. However, Origen's profoundly integrated account of the person differs significantly from the Platonic view. His complex theory of the origin of the created world depicts human bodily existence as a direct consequence and reflection of the condition of preexistent finite minds. We do not receive a generic body, as is the case in the Platonic view. We receive a body with a weight and density that accords with the "negligence of our spirits." "Every created being," Origen writes, "is the result of his own work and his own motive," and our particular place in the hierarchy of created order is "the reward of merit."[38] In other words, for Origen, our bodies are custom tailored to our minds. Moreover, as he speculates on the destiny of finite, embodied creatures, Origen portrays bodily suffering as the preordained means by which God influences our minds and restores us to the perfection necessary for fellowship with Him. He describes the process as the "instruction and training whereby through the flesh the human race, aided by the heavenly powers, is being instructed and trained."[39] Thus, in his analysis of the origin of our bodies and their ongoing significance, Origen closely links body and mind or spirit.

Because Origen so clearly states that our embodiment is a punishment, we tend to think he has a merely negative view of finite existence. This is not, however, the case. God is wise and benevolent, and while the punishment fits the crime, so to speak, it also serves the divine purpose of redemption. According to Origen, one advantage of bodies is that they are plastic and changeable, capable of transformation.[40] As spiritual beings, we are endowed with freedom of choice, and God does not choose to coerce or override that freedom. Were we nothing but spiritual beings, then we would have no hope, because, as sinners, we have freely chosen wickedness. Our fall would be ever downward. However, we are not purely spiritual. We are embodied, and this provides God with an avenue of influence that can effect change in our lives without coercing our wills. Thus, in a crucial passage, Origen writes, "The bodily nature admits of a change in substance, so that God the Artificer of all things, in whatever work of design or construction or restoration he may wish to engage, has at hand the service of this material for all purposes, and can transform and transfer it into whatever forms and species he desires, as the merits of things demand."[41] In short, because we are embodied, we are blessedly subject to the divinely ordained economy of the flesh that can shape and guide our minds.

The difficulty, from our perspective, is that we often experience the economy of the flesh as pain and suffering. Our body chemistry changes, and we get sick. We age and grow feeble. We digest our food and get hungry. The key point, for Origen, is that God so orders and arranges the created world that our bodily suffering has the capacity to encourage us to direct our attention toward God. There is, in other words, a pedagogy of bodies. The world process, "very severe and no doubt full of pain to those who have refused to obey the word of God," provides "instruction and rational training."[42] This training is not verbal or intellectual but is bound up with the entire condition of embodiment. "We must recognize," writes Origen, "that the world was made of such a size and character as to be able to hold all those souls which were destined to undergo discipline in it."[43] God the Artificer of all things sets up the economy of bodies so that we undergo an ascetic training by default. The important question is whether or not we will recognize, embrace, and profit from that discipline.

For this reason, we certainly cannot conclude that the body is unimportant in Origen's theology. The body is decisive because it is the site or location for spiritual discipline. Renunciation of bodily desires does not make a person disembodied; instead, ascetic practice is a form of bodily existence that uses the body in the divinely ordained fashion: to induce progress toward the spiritual. The idea is similar to Augustine's account of the use of finite things. Human existence is embedded in finite, bodily realities, and the goal is not to flee from or deny these realities but to properly engage or use them so that the "mind might be cleansed." The difference is that Augustine pictures the world as an array of potential instruments for spiritual progress that we need to use properly. We are the agents of our own pedagogy. In contrast, for Origen, God is the agent who uses the created order to discipline human beings. Origen has a cosmocentric rather than anthropocentric perspective; it is an approach that adopts a metaphysical interpretation of Irenaeus' more sequential or historical idea of a divine economy that structures all created reality. From this cosmocentric perspective, Origen speculates that God has established an economy of bodily existence that puts pressure on our finite lives, and that pressure, experienced as suffering, drives us upward, toward the spiritual. Thus, Origen weaves the ascetic ideals of Christianity into the very fabric of creation. He understands our embodiment to have a redemptive logic. That we feel pangs of hunger, for example, does not necessarily distract us from spiritual truths; those pangs can provide an occasion or goad toward our true end, which is contemplation.

Origen's genius as a systematic thinker is not to be found in his speculative theology of the creation and consummation of the world. The genius is in

Origen's ability to establish links across various dimensions of thought. In this instance, as we return to the theme of spiritual discipline in relation to scriptural interpretation, Origen links his thoughts about finite, bodily existence with the literal, carnal sense of scripture. He does so at many levels, first by noting the parallel structure of scriptural and human reality, and then by identifying an ascetic economy of scripture that follows the larger ascetic economy of creation. The literality of scripture, he argues, works to pressure readers toward contemplation of God.[44]

Scripture, Origen observes, has three levels or aspects. The first, he writes, "we may call the body of scripture (for such is the name we many give to the common and literal interpretation)." We are no more to rest in this bodily sense than we are to simply affirm our bodily desires. This bodily sense is the basis for progress toward the second level of scripture, which Origen calls "the soul of scripture." Here, he means the moral or edifying sense that would lead readers to commit themselves to the right course of life. However, for Origen, scripture does more than exhort. It also reveals the hidden mysteries of God, and it does so at a third level that he associates with the mind or spirit. The upshot, then, is a view of scripture that corresponds to the view of the human condition. "Just as man, therefore, is said to consist of body, soul and spirit, so also does the holy scripture, which has been bestowed by the divine bounty for man's salvation."[45]

In most of Origen's discussion of scripture, like his discussion of human reality, the middle or soul level drops out. The drama of human life takes place within the bodily realm that God arranges and directs in order to guide us toward the truths of the spirit. There is a disciplining, ascetic logic to creaturely, finite existence. The same holds for scripture. Interpretation takes place within the literal sense of the text that God has arranged so as to direct readers toward the spiritual sense. The literal sense, then, has a disciplining, ascetic logic. What is important for our purposes is the correspondence and overlap between the two disciplining processes. We can see this interaction in two ways. First, like so many of the church fathers, Origen insists that ascetic discipline is crucial to proper interpretive method. Second and more uniquely, Origen shows how the literal sense of scripture, like the bodily world created and governed by God, has an ascetic economy.

In the prologue to his *Commentary on the Song of Songs*, Origen gives clear expression to the need for spiritual maturity to control interpretation. We have already discussed Origen's concern that the racy love poetry of the Song of Songs might lead carnal readers astray. Readers who have failed to discipline their sexual desires are likely to dwell upon the erotic images in their purely literal sense. Of such a bodily reader, Origen warns, "If he does not know how to listen to the names of love purely and with chaste ears, he may twist everything he has heard from the inner man to the outer and fleshly man and be turned away from the Spirit to the flesh." The result will be regress in the spiritual life, not progress, for the eroticism of the Song of Songs will cause him to be "impelled and moved to the lusts of the flesh." In other words, if you are preoccupied with sex, then you are very likely to see sex and little else in the Song of Songs. "For this reason," Origen writes, "I give warning and advice to everyone who is not yet free from the vexations of flesh and blood and who has not withdrawn from the desire for corporeal nature that he completely abstain from reading this book and what is said about it."[46] A lack of spiritual discipline can be exegetically dangerous!

Who then ought to read the Song of Songs? According to Origen, those mature in the Christian life have sufficient spiritual discipline to read rightly. Echoing Hebrews 5:14 and 1 Corinthians 3:1–2, Origen reports that the Song of Songs can be as solid food for the perfect, those who have been trained to distinguish good from evil. These readers will know that the literal descriptions of love in the Song of Songs are not to be taken in their literal sense but should be interpreted spiritually as pertaining to the love of the soul or the church for the bridegroom, who is the Word of God.

For Origen and all the church fathers, the training necessary to avoid carnal titillation and move toward spiritual meaning comes from the ascetic disciplines endorsed by the Christian community. However, it is part of Origen's genius that he identifies a disciplining logic within the scriptural text itself. He does not point to obvious passages such as Paul's warning against touching women in 1 Corinthians 7:1. The ascetic economy of scripture is not didactic. Instead, Origen identifies structural and textual forms of discipline. In the case of the Song of Songs, he dwells on the order of the three books ascribed to Solomon: Proverbs, Ecclesiastes, and Song of Songs. The first, he reports, concerns "the subject of morals, setting regulations for life together, as was fitting, in concise and brief maxims." To use Origen's categories, this is a bodily book in which the literal sense guides readers on the path toward righteousness. The second, Ecclesiastes, provides instruction about "natural things," and "by distinguishing them as empty and vain from what is useful and necessary, he warns that vanity must be abandoned and what is useful and right be pursued."[47] This second book of Solomon is thus taken by Origen to be written at the level of the soul. It provides guidance toward the right path, not in each verse according to the literal sense but in its overall demonstration of the vanity of temporal things.

According to Origen, these two books are providentially placed before Song of Songs in the canon of scripture because the reader must pass through these stages of spiritual development in order to properly read the third and final book of Solomon. For the Song of Song concerns itself with contemplative or spiritual truths in which Solomon "urges upon the soul the love of the heavenly and the divine under the figure of the bride and the bridegroom, teaching us that we must attain fellowship with God by the paths of loving affection and of love."[48] Thus, the very order of the books in scripture provides a pedagogy of interpretation, bringing readers through a process of maturation that makes them capable of properly interpreting the spiritual sense.

The journey of Christian maturation involves an ascent toward the spiritual, but as Origen makes clear in his discussion of bodily existence in *On First Principles*, God orchestrates this pedagogy in and through bodily suffering. In other accounts of the pedagogy of scripture, Origen strikes the same note. The paths of scripture do not always ascend happily from level to level, as his account of the relationship between Proverbs, Ecclesiastes, and Song of Songs would seem to suggest. Spiritual discipline, for Origen, has a painful, bitter aspect. The way toward spiritual understanding is narrow.

Origen expounds this narrow way by returning our attention to the distinction, ubiquitous among the church fathers, between the clear, literal sense of scripture and the hidden, obscure spiritual sense. Many modern readers find the notion of hidden meanings difficult to accept. What possible reason could God have to hide his truths? We think that if God wanted to teach us something, then he would say it directly and plainly. For Origen, such a thought is spiritually naïve. Divine wisdom, he argues, has made the scriptures difficult to interpret for the same reason that the world is set up according to an ascetic logic—so that the project of interpretation might be a properly disciplining exercise of every fiber of the reader's being. "The aim," writes Origen of this divine plan of revealing the mysteries within the bodily sense of scripture, "was that not everyone who wished should have these mysteries laid before his feet to trample upon, but that they should be for the man who has devoted himself to studies of this kind with the utmost purity and sobriety and through nights of watching."[49] Anyone who would object that Origen makes the spiritual meaning of scripture something inaccessible to the ordinary man has missed the point. For Origen, God does not want us to be ordinary, for ordinary men and women are preoccupied with bodily life. God wishes us to become perfect, and to make us so, he has laid out a way toward his truth that requires us to devote ourselves tirelessly to the task of interpretation.

Not only are the spiritual truths of scripture hidden. For Origen, scripture teaches its readers how to interpret spiritually by creating a form of bodily suffering born of the apparent futility of the literal sense. "Divine wisdom," he observes, "has arranged for certain stumbling blocks and interruptions of the historical sense . . . by inserting in the midst a number of impossibilities and incongruities, in order that the very interruption of the narrative might as it were present a barrier to the reader and lead him to refuse to proceed along the pathway of the ordinary meaning."[50] Origen collects a great list of passages from scripture to illustrate the pain one feels at the thought of affirming the literal sense. Some are patently "mythological" or anthropomorphic (for example, the passage in Genesis that speaks of God walking in paradise), some are culturally limited aspects of scripture (for example, Jesus' commandment to his disciples not to own shoes), and some are morally repugnant (Origen refers to a verse in the Septuagint that would seem to require uncircumcised boys to be destroyed).[51] In another example, Origen points out how difficult it is to see how the elaborate Old Testament instructions for the construction and decoration of the tabernacle could have significance for Christian faith. Working out the significance in any detail is, writes Origen, "a very difficult, not to say impossible task."[52] He could have adduced many more examples, for the stumbling blocks of scripture are many.

The bodily sense of scripture, for Origen, is recalcitrant, difficult, and obscure, and if the interpreter believes that it is the divine word, then the result will be a painful grimace of suffering. It is as if Origen had anticipated the experience of every pious student who, having enrolled in a course in modern biblical studies, is confronted by a professor who spends a great deal of time showing just how badly the Bible fits with his inherited faith. This experience naturally evokes a Job-like question. "Why has God so organized his witness that the more I learn about it, the more difficult it is to make sense of it?" For Origen, the answer is simple. To know the languages, to be capable of memorizing the text, to have intellectual ability, even to possess the rule of faith, is not enough. We interpret truly when we see that the scriptural text teaches the mystery of God and the carnal eye cannot see the brightness of the holiness of God. For this reason, the scriptures humiliate and parry interpretive effort so that "by shutting us out and debarring us from [literal reading, they] recall us to the beginning of another way, and might thereby bring us, though the entrance of a narrow footpath, to a higher and loftier road and lay open the immense breadth of the divine wisdom."[53] Reading is difficult because God wants us to suffer the dry deserts of incomprehension as so many days of interpretive fasting. Thus disciplined by the body of scripture, our vision is sanctified and prepared for us to enter into the narrow footpath.

For Origen, the pedagogy of scripture guides readers to an asceticism of carnal interpretive desire that corresponds to and reinforces the broad Christian project of bodily discipline. We must renounce our desire for a solution to the great crossword puzzle of scripture that is based upon a literal reading. "The Spirit has mingled not a few things by which the historical narrative is interrupted and broken," Origen writes, as if anticipating modern judgments about the accuracy of scripture, "with the object of turning and calling the attention of the reader, by the impossibility of the literal sense, to an examination of the inner meaning."[54] Indeed, for Origen, because God is incomprehensible, we must see that the puzzle itself is ordained by God, not to be solved but to focus our minds and lives on a solution that cannot be arrived at or possessed as a conclusion. Such is his ascetic pedagogy that disciplines interpretive desire so that readers will be driven into the "narrow openings" of scripture, "to be flooded with the brightness of immeasurable light."[55]

Origen's ability to coordinate an account of created reality, human existence, and the nature of scripture according to a common ascetic logic is remarkable. However, the notion that exegesis fosters and flows from a disciplined life was as universal in the early church as his genius was unique. In the first of his famous *Theological Orations*, Gregory of Nazianzus meditates upon the nature of theology, which he takes to be the discipline of thought that emerges from the formation of the mind in accordance with scripture. "It is not for all men," he writes, "but only for those who have been tested and have found a sound footing in study, and, more importantly, have undergone, or at the very least are undergoing, purification of body and soul." Gregory's emphasis upon purification testifies to the ambition of patristic interpretation. The goal of exegesis, for Gregory and for the tradition as a whole, is not worldly knowledge but divine wisdom. This goal stretches the reader toward God, and the danger is not that one might arrive at the wrong conclusions. "For one who is not pure to lay hold of pure things," concludes Gregory, "is dangerous, just as it is for weak eyes to look at the sun's brightness."[56] Vision must be sanctified if one is to see rather than be blinded by the mystery of God.

Notes

ONE: Scriptural Meaning Modern to Ancient

1. See Henry Chadwick's classic, *The Early Church* (London: Penguin, 1967), revised 1993.

2. As an example of this approach, see Elizabeth Clark, *The Origenist Controversy: The Cultural Construction of an Early Christian Debate* (Princeton: Princeton University Press, 1992), and for a summary of the state of scholarly debate, David Brakke, "The Early Church in North America: Late Antiquity, Theory, and the History of Christianity," *Church History* 71, no. 3 (September 2002): 473–91.

3. J. N. D. Kelly, *Early Christian Doctrines* (New York: Harper & Row, 1960).

4. Christopher Stead, *Philosophy in Christian Antiquity* (Cambridge: Cambridge University Press, 1994).

5. David Brakke, *Athanasius and the Politics of Asceticism* (New York: Oxford University Press, 1995).

6. See, e.g., Manilo Simonetti, *Biblical Interpretation in the Early Church: An Historical Introduction to Patristic Exegesis*, trans. John A. Hughes (Edinburgh: T. & T. Clark, 1994); Frances Young, *Biblical Exegesis and the Formation of Christian Culture* (Cambridge: Cambridge University Press, 1997), Robert M. Grant and David Tracy, *A Short History of the Interpretation of the Bible* (Philadelphia: Fortress Press, 1984), James L. Kugel and Rowan A. Greer, *Early Biblical Interpretation* (Philadelphia: Westminster Press, 1986), David Dawson, *Allegorical Readers and Cultural Revision in Ancient Alexandria* (Berkeley: University of California Press, 1992). There are also a growing number of scholarly articles tackling specific figures and issues. See, e.g., the collections, *Augustine and the Bible*, ed. A.-M. La Bonnardière, ed. and trans. Pamela Bright (Notre Dame: University of Notre Dame Press, 1999) and *The Bible in Christian Greek Antiquity*, ed. and trans. Paul M. Blowers (Notre Dame: University of Notre Dame Press, 1997).

7. See, e.g., *Against the Heresies*, 1.14.

8. Ibid., 3.11.8.

9. John J. O'Keefe, "'A Letter that Killeth': Toward a Reassessment of Antiochene Exegesis, or Diodore, Theodore, and Theodoret on the Psalms," *Journal of Early Christian Studies* 8, no. 1: 83–104.

10. The most important was Hans W. Frei, *The Eclipse of Biblical Narrative: A Study in Eighteenth and Nineteenth Century Hermeneutics* (New Haven: Yale University Press, 1974). See also, Sandra Schneiders, *The Revelatory Text: Interpreting the New Testament as Sacred Scripture* (San Francisco: Harper, 1991); Frances Young, *The Art of Performance* (London: Darton, Longman and Todd, 1990).

11. See *On Christian Doctrine*, 3.27–28.

12. See the theological sections in Brevard S. Childs, *The Book of Exodus: A Critical, Theological Commentary* (Philadelphia: Westminster, 1974).

13. *Against the Heresies*, 2.28.2.

14. *On First Principles*, 4.1.6.

15. Rowan Greer recognizes some of the same difficulties, although he does not explain the role of theories of meaning: "If we are to understand the ancient Church's use of Scripture, we must learn to suspend our modern expectations" (*Early Biblical Interpretation* [Philadelphia: Westminster Press, 1986], 112).

16. *Life of Moses*, 1.24.

17. For an example of an attempt to assimilate Gregory's interpretation of the *theoria* to modern assumptions about meaning, consult Herbertus Mursurillo, "History and Symbol," *Theological Studies* 18 (1957): 357–86. See also R. M. Grant, *The Letter and the Spirit* (London: 1957), 125.

18. *Life of Moses*, 2.12.

19. Ibid., 2.27.

20. Ibid., 2.31.

21. Ibid., 2.32–34.

22. Ibid., Prologue.15.

23. See Anthony Meredith, S.J., *Gregory of Nyssa* (London: Routledge, 1999).

24. For the interest in typology as a precursor to modern interests in history, see G. W. H. Lampe, and K. J. Woollcombe, *Essays in Typology* (London: SCM Press, 1957). For the more speculative fascination with typology, see Erich Auerbach, "Figura," in *Scenes from the Drama of European Literature*, ed. Wlad Godzich and Jochen Schulte-Sasse (Minneapolis: University of Minnesota Press, 1984).

25. *Commentary on the Psalms*, see the interpretation of Psalm 29.

26. Ibid., 80, 1062–70.

27. *Life of Moses*, 2.189–201.

28. Ibid., 2.190.

29. *On Christian Doctrine*, 1.10.

TWO: Christ Is the End of the Law and the Prophets

1. For a discussion of the common project of a unified reading and some subtle differences within it, see Morweena Ludlow, "Theology and Allegory: Origen and Gregory of Nyssa on the Unity and Diversity of Scripture," *International Journal of Systematic Theology* 4, no. 1 (March 2002): 45–66.

2. *Ephesians* 6:1.

3. *Philadelphians* 7:2.

4. There has been significant scholarly debate about the meaning of the term *archives* in this context. The general consensus is that the term refers to the books of the Old Testament. See William R. Schoedel, *Ignatius of Antioch: A Commentary on the Letter of Ignatius of Antioch* (Philadelphia: Fortess, 1985), 207.

5. All quotes from *Philadelphians* 8:2.

6. The commentary may be found in *Sources Chrétiennes*, no. 244, *Sur la Genèse II*, ed. Pierre Nautin (Paris: Les éditions du cerf, 1976), 137–41.

7. *Against the Heresies*, Preface.1.

8. The role of classical rhetorical training in patristic theology was identified in a nineteenth-century study by Edwin Hatch, *The Influence of Greek Ideas on Christianity* (reprint, New York: Harper, 1957). The connections between classical rhetoric and patristic interpretation are detailed in Francis Young, "The Rhetorical Schools and Their Influence on Patristic Exegesis," *The Making of Orthodoxy: Essays in Honour of Henry Chadwick*, ed. Rowan Williams (Cambridge: Cambridge University Press, 1989).

9. In what follows, we rely on the lucid discussion in Robert M. Grant, *Irenaeus of Lyon* (London: Routledge, 1997), 47–51.

10. For a clear and effective presentation of the basic elements of the ancient view as it applies to Irenaeus, see Grant, 47–49. For a discussion of the relationship of the term *hypothesis* to the later term *skopos,* see the discussion in Young, 190–93.

11. *Against the Heresies,* 1.8.1.

12. Ibid., 1.9.4.

13. Ibid., 3.16.6.

14. Ibid., 1.22.1.

15. Ibid., 3.3.3.

16. Ibid., 5.11.1.

17. Irenaeus rehearses the forms of recapitulation in *Against the Heresies,* 5.19.

18. Ibid., 1.10.3.

19. Ibid., 5.1.1.

20. Ibid., 4.26.1.

21. *Dialogue with Trypho,* 29.

22. Ibid., 44.

23. See, e.g., Robert L. Wilken, "St. Cyril of Alexandria: The Mystery of Christ in the Bible," *Pro Ecclesia* 4, no. 4 (Fall 1995): 454–78.

24. *Treatise on the Mysteries,* vol. 1, Preface.

THREE: Intensive Reading

1. See Harry Gamble, *Books and Readers in the Early Church* (New Haven: Yale University Press, 1995).

2. For accounts of this legend, see Ireneaus, *Against the Heresies,* 3.21.1, and Augustine, *City of God,* 18.42.

3. *Treatise on the Passover,* 1:5–10.

4. Ibid., 1:32–6.

5. Ibid., 2:10.

6. Ibid., 14:25.

7. Ibid., 14:17–28.

8. Ibid., 26:5ff.

9. *Commentary on the Gospel According to John,* 1.90.

10. Ibid., 1.91.

11. Ibid., 1.95.

12. Ibid., 1.103.

13. Ibid., 1.104.

14. Ibid., 1.106.

15. Ibid., 1.111.

16. For background on this controversy, see R. P. C. Hanson, *The Search for the Christian*

Doctrine of God (Edinburgh: T. & T. Clark, 1988), and Rowan Williams, *Arius: Heresy and Tradition* (reprint, Grand Rapids: Eerdmans, 2002).

17. See Plato's dialogue, *The Sophist*: "Dividing according to kinds, not taking the same form for a different one or a different one for the same—is not that the business of the science of dialectic?" (253d).

18. *Orations against the Arians*, 2.7.

19. For an attempt to show that the development of Nicene doctrine stemmed from exegetical judgments and provides a framework for an integrative reading of the scriptures as a whole, see John Behr, *The Way to Nicea: Formation of Christian Theology,* vol. 1 (Crestwood: St. Vladimir's Seminary Press, 2001).

20. *Commentary on the Gospel of John*, Preface.

21. Ibid.

22. *Homilies on Genesis*, Homily 13.3.

23. "On the Interpretation of Scripture," *Essays and Reviews* (London: John W. Parker and Son, 1860), 37.

FOUR: Typological Interpretation

1. *Homilies on Genesis,* 10.8.

2. *Dialogue,* 75.

3. Ibid., 111.

4. Ibid.

5. Ibid., 113.

6. Ibid.

7. Ibid.

8. Ibid.

9. Ibid., 114.

10. Ibid.

11. *Homilies on Joshua,* 1.3.

12. Ibid.

13. Ibid., 1.7.

14. This explains the enthusiastic interest in patristic typology among modern historical scholars. For example, A. C. Charity, *Events and their Afterlife: The Dialectics of Christian Typology in the Bible and Dante* (Cambridge: Cambridge University Press, 1966). See also Lampe and Woollcombe, *Essays in Typology.*

15. *Mystagogical Lectures,* 1.2.

16. Ibid., 1.3.

17. Ibid., 2.2.

18. Ibid., 2.4.

19. Ibid., 2.5.

20. Bertrand de Margerie, *An Introduction to the History of Exegesis,* vol. 1, *The Greek Fathers,* trans. Lenord Maluf (Petersham, MA: Saint Bede's Publications, 1993), 8–9.

21. *Romans,* 3.2.

22. Ibid., 7.2.

23. *Martyrdom of Polycarp,* 22.1.

24. Marcus Borg, *Jesus of New Vision* (New York: HarperCollins, 1991).

25. Ibid., 8.

26. Ibid., 15.

27. Rudolph Otto, *The Idea of the Holy,* trans. John W. Harvey (London and New York: Oxford University Press, 1973). Mircea Eliade was a prolific writer, but *The Sacred and the Profane,* translated by Willard R. Trask (New York: Harper and Row, 1961), provides a good introduction to his ideas.

28. Borg, 57.

29. Ibid., 15.

30. Ibid., 16.

31. Ibid., 191, 192.

32. Lampe and Woollcombe, 17–18.

FIVE: Allegorical Interpretation

1. See Daniel Boyarin, *A Radical Jew: Paul and the Politics of Identity* (Berkeley: University of California Press, 1994).

2. See David Dawson, *Figural Reading and the Fashioning of Christian Identity* (Berkeley: University of California Press, 2002).

3. http://www.hermes-press.com/cas1.htm, accessed January 6, 2004.

4. See Edwin Honig, *The Dark Conceit: The Making of Allegory* (Evanston: Northwestern University Press, 1959).

5. *Literal Commentary on Genesis,* 4.3.1.

6. Ibid., 1.10.

7. See Ibid., 1.11.

8. See Ibid., 1.9.

9. See Ibid., 1.17.

10. *On the Making of Man,* 16.

11. Ibid.

12. *Life of Moses,* 1.77.

13. Ibid., 2.22.

14. Ibid., 2.70.

15. Ibid., 2.107.

16. Ibid., 2.108.

17. Ibid.

18. The allegorical project of Neoplatonic interpretation is fully documented in Robert Lamberton, *Homer the Theologian: Neoplatonist Allegorical Reading and Growth of the Epic Tradition* (Berkley: University of California Press, 1986). Of the Neoplatonic reading of Homer he notes on page viii, "On the one hand, these interpreters strove to redeem the reputation of Homer as a bulwark of pagan Greek culture by demonstrating that his stories and the model of reality that could be deduced from them were in fact compatible with contemporary idealist thought. On the other hand, the more exoteric Platonists were simultaneously concerned to make use of Homer's prestige—to whose appeal no Greek could be immune—to bolster the doctrines of later Platonism."

19. *Commentary on the Song of Songs,* Prologue, 1.

20. Ibid., 1.1.

21. Ibid., 1.2.

22. Ibid.

23. Ibid., 1.4.

24. Ibid.

25. R. P. C. Hanson, *Allegory and Event* (reprint, Louisville: Westminster John Knox, 2002).

26. Ibid., 367.

27. Virginia Burrus, *Begotten Not Made: Conceiving Manhood in Late Antiquity* (Stanford: Stanford University Press, 2000).

28. Ibid., 1.

29. Ibid., 3.

30. Ibid., 126–27.

31. Ernst Troeltsch, *The Social Teachings of the Christian Church* (reprint, New York: Harper, 1960).

SIX: The Rule of Faith and the Holy Life

1. *On Christian Doctrine*, Prologue.

2. All quotes from Manilo Simonetti, *Biblical Interpretation in the Early Church: An Historical Introduction to Patristic Exegesis*, trans. John A. Hughes (Edinburgh: T. & T. Clark, 1994), 23–24.

3. *On First Principles*, 4.1.6.

4. Our use of the analogy of scientific research is indebted to Imre Lakatos' description of scientific theory in relation to data. See *The Methodology of Scientific Research Programmes*, ed. John Worral and Gregory Currie (Cambridge: Cambridge University Press, 1978).

5. *Against the Heresies*, 1.10.1.

6. See the long outline of salvation history, ibid., 1.10.3.

7. Ibid., 1.22.1.

8. Ibid., 2.28.2–3.

9. Ibid., 2.27.1.

10. Ibid., 2.28.3.

11. See ibid., 1.9.4.

12. See ibid., 1.8.1.

13. *On Christian Doctrine*, 2.8.

14. Ibid., 2.9.

15. Ibid., 3.2.

16. Ibid.

17. Ibid., 3.10.

18. *Against the Heresies*, 3.1.1.

19. Ibid., 2.27.2.

20. For a helpful discussion of Irenaeus' application of the rule as a framework for interpretation, see Greer, *Early Biblical Interpretation* (Philadelphia: Westminster Press, 1986), 155–76.

21. *Stromata*, 7.16.

22. *Against the Heresies*, 2.28.2.

23. *On First Principles*, 4.2.3.

24. For extensive references see Douglas Burton-Christie, *The Word in the Desert: Scripture and the Quest for Holiness in Early Christian Monasticism* (New York: Oxford University Press, 1993).

25. *On Christian Doctrine*, 1.4.

26. Ibid.

27. Ibid.

28. Ibid., 1.9.

29. Ibid., 1.17.

30. Ibid., 1.5.

31. Ibid., 1.10.

32. See ibid., 1.26.

33. Ibid., 1.36.

34. Ibid., 1.40.

35. *Life of Anthony*, 82.

36. *On First Principles*, Preface.8.

37. Ibid.

38. Ibid., 1.5.3. See also 1.8.1. Preexistent spirits receive angelic, demonic, or human bodies "as a means of punishing each in proportion to its sin." Again in 1.8.2: "The cause of the diversity and variety among [embodied creatures] is shown to be derived not from any unfairness on the part of the Disposer but from their own actions, which exhibit varying degrees of earnestness or laxity according to the goodness and badness of each."

39. *On First Principles*, 1.6.3.

40. See ibid., 2.1.4.

41. Ibid., 3.6.7.

42. Ibid., 2.3.1.

43. Ibid., 3.5.4.

44. Our discussion of the relationship between Origen's speculative theology and biblical interpretation is indebted to David Dawson, *Christian Figural Reading and the Fashioning of Identity* (Berkeley: University of California Press, 2002).

45. *On First Principles*, 4.2.4.

46. All quotes from *Origen: An Exhortation to Martyrdom, Prayer and Selected Works*, trans. Rowan A. Greer (New York: Paulist Press, 1979), 218.

47. *Origen*, 232.

48. Ibid.

49. *On First Principles*, 4.2.7.

50. Ibid., 4.2.9.

51. See ibid., 4.3.1.

52. See ibid., 4.2.2.

53. Ibid., 4.2.9.

54. Ibid.

55. Ibid., 4.2.3.

56. *Theological Orations*, 27.2.

Bibliography

Primary Sources in Translation

In order to facilitate further study of patristic exegesis we have used existing English translations whenever possible.

Athanasius. *Against the Arians. Nicene and Post-Nicene Fathers,* vol. 4. Ed. Philip Schaff. Reprint, Peabody, MA: Hendrickson, 1994.

——. *The Life of Anthony and the Letter to Marcellinus.* Trans. Robert C. Gregg. New York: Paulist, 1980.

——. *On the Incarnation of the Word.* Crestwood, NY: St. Vladimir's Seminary Press, 1996.

Augustine. *Confessions.* Trans. Henry Chadwick. Oxford: Oxford University Press, 1991.

——. *Literal Commentary on Genesis.* Trans. John Hammond Taylor. New York: Newman Press, 1982.

——. *On Christian Doctrine.* Trans. D. W. Robertson. New York: McMillan, 1987.

Cyril of Alexandria. *Commentary on John.* Trans. P. E. Pusey. Oxford, 1874.

Cyril of Jerusalem. *Mystagogical Lectures.* Fathers of the Church, vol. 64. Trans. Leo P. McCauley and Anthony A. Stephenson. Washington, DC: Catholic University of America Press, 1970.

Gregory of Nazinzus. *The Theological Orations.* In *Faith Gives Fullness to Reasoning: The Five Theological Orations of Gregory Nazianzen.* Introduction and commentary by Frederick W. Norris. Trans. Lionel Wickham and Frederick Williams. Leiden: E. J. Brill, 1991.

Gregory of Nyssa. *The Life of Moses.* Trans. Abraham J. Malherbe and Everett Ferguson. New York: Paulist, 1978.

——. *On the Making of Man. Nicene and Post-Nicene Fathers,* vol. 5. Ed. Philip Schaff. Reprint, Peabody, MA: Hendrickson, 1994.

Ignatius of Antioch. *Letters.* In *Early Christian Fathers.* Ed. Cyril C. Richardson. New York: Collier Books, 1970.

Irenaeus of Lyons. *Against the Heresies.* Trans. Dominic J. Unger. New York: Paulist, 1992. Also in *Ante-Nicene Fathers,* vol. 1. Ed. Alexander Roberts and James Donaldson. Reprint, Peabody, MA: Hendrickson, 1994.

John Chrysostom. *Homilies on Genesis.* Fathers of the Church, vol. 74. Trans. Robert C. Hill. Washington, DC: Catholic University of America Press, 1986.

Justin Martyr. *Dialogue with Trypho.* Fathers of the Church, vol. 3. Trans. Thomas B. Falls. Reprint, Washington, DC: Catholic University of America Press, 1977.

The Martyrdom of Polycarp. In *Early Christian Fathers.* Ed. Cyril C. Richardson. New York: Collier Books, 1970.

Origen. *Commentary on the Gospel John*. Fathers of the Church, vols. 80 and 89. Trans. Ronald E. Heine. Washington, DC: Catholic University of America Press, 1989 and 1993.

———. *Commentary on the Song of Songs*. Trans. R. P. Lawson. New York: Newman, 1956.

———. *On First Principles*. Trans. G. W. Butterworth. Reprint, Gloucester, MA: Peter Smith, 1973.

———. *Treatise on the Passover*. Trans. Robert J. Daly. New York: Paulist, 1992.

When not available in English, we have translated from the following critical editions.

Didymus the Blind. *Commentary on Genesis*. Sources Chrétiennes vol. 233. Paris: Cerf, 1976.

Hilary of Poitiers. *Treatise on the Mysteries*. Sources Chrétiennes vol. 19. Paris: Cerf, 1967.

Origen. *Homilies on Joshua*. Source Chrétiennes vol. 71. Paris: Cerf, 1960.

Theodoret of Cyrus. *Commentary on the Psalms*, Patrologia Grecae 80.

Selected Secondary Sources

Aers, David. *Piers Plowman and Christian Allegory*. London, 1975.

Ames, Ruth. *The Fulfillment of the Scriptures: Abraham, Moses, and Piers*. Evanston: Northwestern University Press, 1970.

Astell, Ann. *The Song of Songs in the Middle Ages*. Ithaca: Cornell University Press, 1990.

Auerbach, Erich. *Mimesis*. Princeton: Princeton University Press, 1953.

———. *Scenes from the Drama of European Literature*. Minneapolis: University of Minnesota Press, 1984.

Behr, John. *The Way to Nicea: The Formation of Christian Theology*. Vol. 1. Crestwood, NY: St. Vladimir's Seminary Press, 2001.

Blowers, Paul M., ed. and trans. *The Bible in Greek Christian Antiquity*. Notre Dame: University of Notre Dame Press, 1997.

Borg, Marcus. *Jesus: A New Vision*. San Francisco: HarperCollins, 1991.

Boyarin, Daniel. *A Radical Jew: Paul and the Politics of Identity*. Berkeley: University of California Press, 1994.

Brakke, David. *Athanasius and the Politics of Asceticism*. Baltimore: Johns Hopkins University Press, 1998.

———. "The Early Church in North America: Late Antiquity, Theory, and the History of Christianity." *Church History* 71, no. 3 (September 2002): 473–91.

Burrus, Virginia. *"Begotten not Made": Conceiving Manhood in Late Antiquity*. Stanford: Stanford University Press, 2000.

Burton-Christie, Douglas. *The Word in the Desert: Scripture and the Quest for Holiness in Early Christian Monasticism*. New York: Oxford University Press, 1993.

Chadwick, Henry. *The Early Church*. London: Penguin, 1967.

Charity, A. C. *Events and Their Afterlife: The Dialectics of Christian Typology in the Bible and Dante*. Cambridge: Cambridge University Press, 1966.

Dawson, David. *Allegorical Readers and Cultural Revision in Ancient Alexandria*. Berkeley: University of California Press, 1992.

———. *Christian Figural Reading and the Fashioning of Identity*. Berkeley: University of California Press, 2002.

Eliade, Mircea. *The Sacred and the Profane.* Trans. Willard R. Trask. New York: Harper & Row, 1981.

Fletcher, Angus. *Allegory: The Theory of a Symbolic Mode.* Ithaca: Cornell University Press, 1964.

Fowl, Stephen E., ed. *The Theological Interpretation of Scripture.* Cambridge, MA: Blackwell, 1997.

Frei, Hans W. *The Eclipse of Biblical Narrative: A Study in Eighteenth and Nineteenth Century Hermeneutics.* New Haven: Yale University Press, 1974.

Gamble, Harry. *Books and Readers in the Early Church.* New Haven: Yale University Press, 1995.

Grant, Robert M. *Irenaeus of Lyons.* London: Routledge, 1997.

Grant, Robert M., with David Tracy. *A Short History of the Interpretation of the Bible.* 2d ed. Philadelphia: Fortress Press, 1984.

Handelman, Susan A. *The Slayers of Moses: The Emergence of Rabbinic Interpretation in Modern Literary Theory.* Albany: State University of New York Press, 1982.

Hanson, R. P. C. *Allegory and Event.* Reprint, Louisville: Westminster John Knox, 2002.

———. *The Search for the Christian Doctrine of God.* Edinburgh: T. & T. Clark, 1988.

Hatch, Edwin. *The Influence of Greek Ideas on Christianity.* Reprint, New York: Harper, 1957.

Honig, Edwin. *Dark Conceit: The Making of Allegory.* Evanston: Northwestern University Press, 1959.

Illich, Ivan. *In the Vineyard of the Text: A Commentary on Hugh's Didascalicon.* Chicago: University of Chicago Press, 1993.

Jowett, Benjamin. "On the Interpretation of Scripture." *Essays and Reviews.* London: John W. Parker and Son, 1860.

Kelly, J. N. D. *Early Christian Doctrines.* San Francisco: Harper & Row, 1978.

Lamberton, Robert. *Homer the Theologian: Neoplatonist Allegorical Reading and the Growth of the Epic Tradition.* Berkeley: University of California Press, 1986.

Lampe, G. W. H., and K. J. Woollcomb. *Essays in Typology.* London: SCM Press, 1957.

Lewis, C. S. *The Allegory of Love: A Study in Medieval Tradition.* Reprint, New York: Oxford University Press, 1958.

Lindbeck, George. "Hesychastic Prayer and the Christianizing of Platonism: Some Protestant Reflections." *The Church in the Modern Age.* Grand Rapids: Eerdmans Publishing, 2002.

———. *The Nature of Doctrine.* Philadelphia: Westminster Press, 1984.

———. "Scripture, Consensus and Community." In *Biblical Interpretation in Crisis: The Ratzinger Conference on Bible and Church.* Ed. Richard John Neuhaus. Grand Rapids: Eerdmans Publishing, 1989.

Ludlow, Morweena. "Theology and Allegory: Origen and Gregory of Nyssa on the Unity and Diversity of Scripture." *International Journal of Systematic Theology* 4, no. 1 (March 2002): 45–66.

Margerie, Bertrand de. *An Introduction to the History of Exegesis.* Vol. 1: *The Greek Fathers.* Trans. Lenord Maluf. Petersham, MA: Saint Bede's Publications, 1993.

Marrou, Henri-Irénée. "*Doctrina* et *disciplina* dans la langue des pères de l'Église." *Bulletin du Cange* 10 (1934): 5–25.

O'Keefe, John J. " 'A Letter that Killeth': Toward a Reassessment of Antiochene Exegesis, or Diodore, Theodore, and Theodoret on the Psalms." *Journal of Early Christian Studies* 8, no. 1 (2000): 83–104.

Otto, Rudolph. *The Idea of the Holy.* Trans. John W. Harvey. London: Oxford University Press, 1973.

Prickett, Stephen. *Words and the Word: Language, Poetics and Biblical Interpretation.* Cambridge: Cambridge University Press, 1986.

Schoedel, William R. *A Commentary on the Letters of Ignatius of Antioch.* Philadelphia: Fortress, 1985.

Stead, Christopher. *Philosophy in Christian Antiquity.* Cambridge: Cambridge University Press, 1994.

Torjensen, Karen Jo. *Hermeneutical Procedure and Theological Method in Origen's Exegesis.* Berlin: Walter de Gruyter, 1986.

Trigg, Joseph W. *Origen.* New York: Routledge, 1998.

———. *Origen: The Bible and Philosophy in the Third-Century Church.* Atlanta: John Knox, 1983.

Troeltsch, Ernst. *The Social Teachings of the Christian Church.* Reprint, New York: Harper, 1960.

Wilken, Robert L. "St. Cyril of Alexandria: The Mystery of Christ in the Bible." *Pro Ecclesia* 4, no. 4 (Fall 1995): 454–78.

Williams, Rowan. *Arius: Heresy and Tradition.* Reprint, Grand Rapids: Eerdmans, 2002.

Young, Frances. "The Rhetorical Schools and Their Influence on Patristic Exegesis." In *The Making of Orthodoxy: Essays in Honour of Henry Chadwick.* Ed. Rowan Williams. Cambridge: Cambridge University Press, 1989.

———. *Biblical Exegesis and the Formation of Christian Culture.* Cambridge: Cambridge University Press, 1997.

———. *The Art of Performance: Toward a Theology of Holy Scripture.* London: Darnton, Longman, & Todd, 1990. Also published as *Virtuoso Theology.* Cleveland, OH: Pilgrim Press, 1993.

Index

source and redaction criticism, 10

St. Ignatius of Loyola, 100

symbolism, 10

Targumim, 50

Ten Commandments, 11

Theodoret of Cyrus, 20

Theological Orations (Gregory of Nazianzus), 139

theoria, 15–16, 17–18, 19, 100–101

Timaeus (Plato), 61

Tolkien, J. R. R., 91, 92

Treatise on the Mysteries (Hilary of Poitiers), 42–43

Treatise on the Passover (Origen), 51–53

Trinity, 56–63

Troeltsch, Ernst, 112

Trypho, the Jew, 74, 76

typological exegesis: anticipation of Christ, 73–74; baptism and Exodus, 79–82, 87; criticisms of, 84–85, 87–88; defined, 70; economy of, 85–88; influence upon Christian practice, 78–79; martyrdom, 82–84; New Testament and Old Testament associations, 74–78; strategy, 19–21, 69; unifying factor, 70–74

typology, 19–20, 90

typos, 19

Washington, George, 8, 10